Transformational Church

CREATING A
NEW SCORECARD FOR
CONGREGATIONS

Transformational Church

Ed Stetzer + Thom S. Rainer

B&H
PUBLISHING GROUP

NASHVILLE, TENNESSEE

978-1-4336-6930-9

Published by B&H Publishing Group
Nashville, Tennessee

Dewey Decimal Classification: 260
Subject Heading: CHURCH \ CHURCH GROWTH \
CHURCH RENEWAL

4 5 6 7 8 9 10 • 16 15 14 13 12

This book is dedicated to churches trying and struggling to be on mission in their context—don't give up. God is still working in and through the church.

FROM THOM

To my three grandchildren: Canon, Maggie, and one who will be born shortly after this book is released. In each of you I have great hope and promise.

To Nellie Jo, of course. You always make me smile.

FROM ED

To my three girls: Kristen, Jaclyn, and Kaitlyn. The grace of God I see at work in your lives gives me hope for the future of the church.

To Donna, my wife and best friend. Thanks for the constant joy you bring to my life.

ACKNOWLEDGMENTS

THE TRANSFORMATIONAL CHURCH STUDY is the product of a whole host of people who deserve our thanks.

First is the team at LifeWay Research. Scott McConnell, Director of Research, is a great friend of the church. We appreciate his intellectual ability to interact with the minutia of the data and then see the overarching principles at work in the church. Thanks also to Lizette Beard who served as the Project Manager for the process. Many churches in our study are the beneficiaries of her love for the church and ever-growing desire to see the gospel penetrate our culture. Other members of the LifeWay Research team deserve mention as well. Melissa Kendall, Matt Lowe, Sandra Wilson, and Shirley Cross are indispensable to all we do. Thanks also to Courtney Eichelberger, Melody Raines, Danny Moore, and Melanie Gillen for their work with the team.

We also want to thank our friend Eric Geiger. Early on, Eric took on the task of understanding the initial findings of the survey. His understanding of the church and ability to see the principles emerging from statistical surveys is an uncommon gift among pastors.

Some of the unsung heroes of the Transformational Church study were the church consultants from LifeWay. Led by David Francis, these men and women spent many days traveling our country and interviewing churches. The encouragement they returned with from the field gives us a great hope that the stories told and the principles taught in this book will aid countless churches in the future. Thanks goes to our team: David Trammel, Elgia (Jay) Wells, Doug Merritt, Dan Garland, Larry Golden, Pat Ford, Rusty Richardson, Steve Taylor, Terry Martinaz, Charles Grant, Jeffery Curtis, Renee Hardwick, Chuck Gaines, Eddie Clay, Jim Maddox, Ken Lupton, Richard Edfeldt, Sam Galloway, David Burt, Doug Akers, Sharon Burroughs, Keith Feather, Michael Gentry, Paul Billingsley, Tom Crocker, Barry Sneed, Barry Campbell, Mike Tucker, Diana Frey, and Bill Banks.

We also want to thank Mike Harland, David Francis, Bret Robbe, Bruce Raley, and Rick Howerton for making significant contributions to our thinking about worship (from Mike) and the small-group structure of the church (from David, Bret, and Rick). Also, Dino Senesi, Todd Littleton, Jared Wilson, Trevin Wax, Marty Duren, Chris Brewer, and Matthew Smith provided invaluable input and assistance.

Thomas Walters and the team at B&H Publishing are always at the top of our list of people to thank as well. We are ever grateful and constantly in awe of the work they do to make our writing better so you will benefit from the content of the teaching we hope to impart.

Thanks also to Philip Nation, Director of Ministry Development at LifeWay Research, for his work to help guide the content of this book toward completion. Without Philip, there would be no Transformational Church book.

Thanks to the experts who consulted with us during the quantitative research phase of the project: Alan Hirsch, Chuck Lawless, Elmer Towns, Bob Whitesel, Gary McIntosh, Bill Easum, and Dallas Anderson. We are honored to serve as colleagues in the ministry with these men. But more than that, we are blessed to call them friends.

We spend a lot of time on the road and writing at home. We could not do what we do without the love, support, and patience of our wives. Nellie Jo and Donna deserve so much more than these mere words. We still want our wives to know of our deep love and appreciation for each of them. We are two blessed men.

CONTENTS

1
Hope for Transformation

TRANSFORMATION + CHURCH

For followers of Jesus, these are two of the most important and powerful words in the world.

We treasure the concept of "transformation," because radical change is the heart of the Christian message and because the power of the gospel changes everything—lives, churches, and communities.

Christians love "church," because God has chosen the community of Christ followers to make known His manifold wisdom (Eph. 3:10). When God transforms lives, He doesn't just build temples of the Holy Spirit in individuals, He builds His church by adding more lives to the body. God uses the individuals in the church to bring about the transformation of more individuals and, consequently, the growth of the church. The church is God's tool and instrument for His kingdom agenda.

The concepts of transformation and church play off each other, complement each other, connect to each other. And when you put not just the nouns *transformation* and *church* together (as we have in the title), but put together the actual occurrence of transformation and the community of people called the church, the result is powerful. It's amazing. The result is transformation and church the way God designed them to be.

The truth is that transformation is non-negotiable for the Christian church. But change is not the norm for many of our churches. We are supposed to see transformation, but too often we see stagnation. God's plan is that "We all, with unveiled faces, are reflecting the glory of the Lord and are being transformed into the same image from glory to glory; this is from the Lord who is the Spirit" (2 Cor. 3:18). That means that we (as individuals) and "we all" (as the church) are supposed to see this transformation. Transforming "from glory to glory" should be normal, but too often it is exceptional. Our passion is to help the church see, aspire to, and achieve biblical transformation.

> *We are supposed to see transformation, but too often we see stagnation.*

Our longing to understand how God transforms people and communities through His church led us to undertake this research project—the largest ever of its kind. We, alongside dozens of other leaders, threw ourselves completely into this project in order to better understand how some churches are experiencing this transformation today.

Change

There is no avoiding change. Ever heard the saying "The only constant is change"? It's a truism built upon the reality that change is built into life itself. Most times we don't even have to do anything to bring change about—change just *happens*. Every day we encounter all sorts of new developments, good and bad. No matter what we do, change comes to all of us. In fact, you don't have to do anything. Just sit there; change will find you.

We can't choose whether change will come or not. But we *can* choose whether to embrace it or resist it. We can choose the kind of change that advances the kingdom of God into our world, or we can retreat

> *Our longing to understand how God transforms people and communities through His church led us to undertake this research project—the largest ever of its kind.*

into a subculture that attempts to insulate us *from* the world. In our day we face an opportunity for change that can deliver transformation to individuals, churches, and whole communities. Will we engage? Or will we resist? What will the church do?

We have spent most of our adult lives as leaders serving churches. During those years, like many of you, we have watched God transform people with the power of the gospel. Transformation is at the heart of God's mission to humanity. He delights in moving us from the kingdom of darkness to the kingdom of light—and then empowering and directing us as agents of His kingdom. And He has chosen the church as His instrument in this world. We, the body of Christ, are God's chosen method to deliver the message of transformation to our neighbors both in the local community and around the world. Delivering this message is our mission.

The alternative to this biblically-mandated transformation is to pick a rut and make it deeper. And this is just what many churches have done, preferring, even if not consciously, repetition or even stagnation. As leaders, we sometimes fool ourselves into thinking that just managing the status quo is good enough. Some leaders take the merry-go-round approach to church. They think if they can just keep everyone moving, the flashing lights shining bright, and the music happy, they won't get any complaints. Some leaders try to take the "don't rock the boat" approach. They think that if we all remain very still in the boat, it won't turn over. But it also won't go anywhere.

> *Rather than missionary disciples for Christ going into the world, we have a group of people content to go in circles.*

The big problem? Whether still or busy, too few are making any real headway. Rather than missionary disciples for Christ going into the world, we have a group of people content to go in circles. God calls us to make a transformational impact on the world, not provide a carnival of frenetic activity for ourselves. But to make this impact, we must engage in His mission for His sake and on His terms. Pastors and church leaders must move beyond entertaining consumers and into engaging Christ's mission.

We believe that God is not done with the church—He is continuing His work. Right now it's en vogue to look down on the church. If you take a look at certain sections of the blog and book worlds, or just peruse the Christian Twittersphere, you can find all kinds of people taking all kinds of shots at the Bride of Christ. And they're doing it for all kinds of reasons. Many are disillusioned with the church of their upbringing. Some are discouraged by decline or scandals. A younger generation is frustrated with the church's apparent apathy about social justice causes. Some are upset that the church won't get more modernized; some are upset because the church has lost its ancient ways. There are criticisms abounding of emerging churches, seeker churches, missional churches, traditional churches, Boomer churches, multi-site churches, old churches, new churches, and the list goes on. Sometimes it seems there are as many complaints as there are Christians, and some of these complaints are well meaning.

But in any event, the response to transformational inactivity for many Christians appears to just be criticism. If you can't do, teach. And if you can't do *or* teach, become a critic. For all kinds of reasons and with all kinds of motives, many are swinging away at the church like a low hanging piñata on Cinco-de-Mayo. Yet despite the beating Christ's Bride is taking, despite the daily write-offs she receives, God is not finished with His church. Far from it.

In Philippians, Paul speaks to the church and says, "I am sure of this, that He who started a good work in you will carry it on to completion until the day of Christ Jesus" (Phil. 1:6). Although we often make this a verse about us, individually, it is about the church as well—God started the work, He is working in the church now, and He will someday finish the work. It is, after all, His church. And, we are "partners . . . in grace" (Phil. 1:7) now, sharers and bearers of the grace that brings transformation. For Spirit-filled believers, there is no more compelling mission, and this mission is what drives the body of Christ. What we lack, keeping us from moving from ruts and routines to transformational mission, is the clarity of focus that comes from finding the grace of God more enthralling and exciting than anything else.

A Personal Mission

You may not think so, but we all know what a mission is like. We all know what it's like to be on a mission. When you're on one, your focus is consuming.

I remember when my (Thom's) first grandchild was born. It was absolutely incredible to watch the transformation in my wife when we got the phone call that our daughter-in-law Rachel was in labor. They live in Wake Forest, North Carolina, and it was too late at night to catch a flight.

But Nellie Jo said anyway, "Let's go."

I said, "You're not packed."

She said, "I'll pack right now."

I'm thinking, *I have three, six, eight hours to wait.* But twenty minutes later she says, "I'm ready. What's wrong with you?"

I said, "We'll never make it in time. It's a good eight- or nine-hour drive over the mountains, and we're going to be traveling all night."

She says, "I'll drive. I don't trust your driving at nighttime."

At this point, I'm thinking about all the trips we've made in the past. I am remembering all the stops for sodas, shopping, and stretching our legs. I was anticipating this eight- to nine-hour trip would turn out to be a twelve- to fifteen-hour marathon. But I was wrong. We made the trip with only one ten-minute stop. Nine hours we drove, in the dark of night. We didn't make it in time for our grandchild's birth, but we arrived shortly thereafter. How'd we defy the odds and the customs of the past to achieve something so amazing? We were on a mission. And when you are on a mission, you get focused.

When we embarked upon the Transformational Church initiative, we wanted to go somewhere. In one sense we wanted to get there fast. But in another sense we wanted to get there properly. Along this journey we have discovered that the mission of some churches becomes complicated by distractions, accidents, and disasters. But we were also able to witness the successful journey many churches are making. The goal of a Transformational Church is to make disciples, and nothing will deter them from this task. Though roadblocks and hazards abound, these churches find ways to stay on track. They are able to bring about a convergence of values and activities that results in transformation of individuals and of the community.

We believe that what is taking place is a viral movement of transformation. People possess a deep hunger for change. On the surface, it shows up with job changes, buying a new car, or finding a new hobby. Superficially, this simply shows the restless nature of humanity. Spiritually, this evidences each soul's God-shaped hole. When churches are spinning their wheels, they are merely reflecting their superficial restlessness. But when churches move forward on God's mission, they engage our spiritual restlessness, the sort of untapped anxiousness inside that is eager and waiting to respond to the command, "Come, follow Me."

The churches we discovered in this initiative share the desire for transformation—but on a deeper level than most churches. Where many churches desire to make a difference, Transformational Churches actually do. They possess an increasing awareness for the need of change in the people, the church, and the community.

Now, before you conclude this is simply another methodology book, keep reading. Although you will encounter numerous practices from Transformational Churches, these practices do not take shape in formulaic packages. Biblical practices transcend cookie-cutter copying. For example, when we report the particular way a church in South Dakota prays together, the principle to take away is that the church in South Dakota connects with God in authentic prayer. The real focus is not the particular way they pray together but the reality that they are praying together. While we showcase the method, we mean to recommend the principle inside it.

Too often the church has become a symbol of gathering for one another rather than scattering for the sake of others. The church was designed by God to be on the move in the world, not sitting in the corner of the neighborhood waiting for the needy to show up on its doorstep. The Bible casts Christians as a *mobilizing* people. And what happens in the individual life of a Christian should happen in the church at large, right? Furthermore, what happens in the church should happen in the community. The lives of believers should authenticate the message we proclaim and the ministries we engage. The alternative authentication is typically more church programming, which gives the illusion of mission. But activity is not always productivity, and in fact in today's church it seldom is.

Our ministry passion is simple: to get God's people on mission. It's why we write and speak on church revitalization, the missional church, and even church planting. All of these matter, but they are the results, not the mechanism. Transformation is the mechanism and the gospel is the means. The gospel is itself power; Paul says it bears fruit and grows (Col. 1:6). The gospel changes us, our churches, and then the world. That's why it matters and matters most.

> **The Bible casts Christians as a mobilizing people.**

Unfortunately, many of you reading this book may not feel like you are in a Transformational Church. Nellie Jo's determination in our first visit with our grandson may strike you as entertaining but not illustrative of your church at all. Perhaps you found more resonance in my (Thom's) seeing our journey as daunting and difficult; the idea of the passive church sitting on the corner of the neighborhood intersection seems to descrbe your current ministry. But it does not have to be. You can engage in God's mission of transformation.

Now for the News

Many of us have been the bearers of bad news. We have spoken and written about the problematic state of North American churches. And there is no reason to be unrealistic about the situation now. There's no ignoring the facts. Conversion growth is declining. The cultural influence of local churches is waning. Leadership in churches is often embattled.

Small-group participation, including Sunday School, is struggling. The evangelistic efforts of the church at large and the leadership of the church are below minimal. These are sad statistics, and solutions to the problems are in short supply.

The rapid decline of mainline denominations is so well documented it seems inappropriate to continue calling them mainline. Evangelical churches have struggled, currently hoping to manage their decline while searching for some magic bullet. Many churches navigate distress and fractures in their fellowship every day. Almost weekly, pastors or other staff persons face forced termination. The statistics on pastoral burnout and depression and moral failings are alarming. We have churches filled with knowledgeable religious people not living on mission, wasting their time criticizing those who are. Churches today know too well about pain. We could go on, but there is little reason to do so. You know the situation—and perhaps it is reflected in the circumstances of your own local church.

You know the problems. Many people are asking, "Does anybody have a word from God on this?" "Is there any hope?" "Is the North American church in such dire straits that all we can do is just prepare for our own death?" "Do we need to scrap what we've got and move on to something else?"

No.

We must not give in to the idea that the church will die. That idea is simply not biblical. And it certainly is not God's plan. But while bad news abounds, the good news is that we see the opposite: positive, productive, fruitful trends in many Transformational Churches.

Through the Transformational Church initiative and study, we have cause for great hope. The men and women who surveyed thousands of pastors and church members encountered unabashed optimism about what God is doing in the church today. The hope we discovered in these churches is the reason we are encouraged about the Transformational Church initiative.

We do not deny the realities of the well-documented statistics about the church in America. In fact, this research initiative confirmed quantitatively what we all thought to be true. The majority of churches are struggling to make a transformational impact on people and communities. But we found something exciting woven throughout the research results. There are gleams of light in the shadows. We hear a hopeful sound coming from some churches across North America.

The Transformational Churches we found are the bearers of hope for our church leaders and all believers.

As our consultants traveled across the United States, they accumulated data from objective surveys. This data gives us reason to be excited about what is possible in the days ahead. In this research, we can see the possibilities of what God can do in local churches.

> *The Transformational Churches we found are the bearers of hope for our church leaders and all believers.*

You hold in your hands the first part of the Transformational Church initiative led by LifeWay Research. It is a compilation of work done over a long period of time by dozens of people and thoroughly reviewed by our research team. But it will not stand on its own. We are dedicated to helping the church succeed, and to that end this book is only the beginning of the process.

We Believe in the Church

We have made our commitment to the local church. This is our commitment, and we hope it is your commitment as well. Why? Because the church is God's instrument to deliver the message of transformation to our communities and to the world. In the Bible we see that God's favor rests on the church and that He has made His commitment to the church in the form of His covenant, so we have decided to invest wherever God has His focus.

We hope to leverage our research, work, and lives for the purpose of building up God's church for God's mission of transforming people with the gospel. We have hope because we are seeing churches that are being transformed by the power of God. As a result, we are seeing transformed lives and communities. Admittedly, the churches we feature are small in number. They are a sample, but they are representative of many more. And while they don't constitute a majority, they are beacons of hope.

A Transformational Church is not simply a "good church" or a church that does good things. Neither is it necessarily a big church that offers excellent programming, preaching, and worship. A TC focuses stubbornly on the gospel's ability to change people. It sees results appropriate for its context and holds the right values that support

> *A TC focuses stubbornly on the gospel's ability to change people.*

transforming mission. A TC has figured out that transformation is much more than a better church strategy.

A TC is more than a group of people who believe Christianity is the right choice and that it offers a better way to live. We found hope in them because they are covenant communities holding to a belief that God will radically change lives and entire communities. They are churches with an optimism about God's limitless abilities. Jim Herrington describes transformation as "an inside-out and downside-up process." He says this about the church:

> "It is about reaching a critical mass of believers who are so empowered by the gospel of Christ that they change everything they touch—family, workplace, schools, business. As this critical mass is achieved, the power of the living God brings significant changes in the problems that plague our cities today—poverty, crime, addictions, gangs, divorce, violence—and a dramatic increase in things that characterize the kingdom of God—mercy, justice, prosperity (especially for the poor) and compassion."[1]

The change we seek is the change that ultimately matters—of individuals, of churches, and of society. When people are changed, churches are changed and communities are changed. This is a stark and biblical contrast to merely changing gears in one's programming or systems, shuffling

Christians around to new modes of activity. If such programs and systems really serve to send out the church on transforming mission of neighbors and neighborhoods, they are on the right track for a TC. But if they are just means of galvanizing enthusiasm for the same pool of believers who participate in every cycle, nothing is really being transformed. (Actually, instead, this cycle of moving from programmatic enthusiasm to enthusiasm can lead to burnout and disillusionment for many Christians.)

Gospel change has always led to broader change. The gospel's power reaches into all nooks and crannies, soaks into all places, plants seeds, and bears fruit. It changes everything. We see this in revivals and reformations throughout history, but the Welsh Revival is one powerful example. In Wales in 1904, God used a young coal miner's burden for revival, a burden he'd carried since childhood, to transform an entire region. Owen Roberts's compassionate love for people led to his calling Christians to commit to listen to God, to be changed by His power, and to live a public faith. As more and more Welsh believers heeded the call, God seized upon the submissive spirit of the church in Wales, and Roberts's burden and love for those outside of the faith inspired an evangelistic and missional fervor unlike they'd ever seen. Malcolm McDow and Alvin Reid write:

> "As God answered this burden, even the newspapers published the results. In two months, 70,000 were converted, 85,000 in five months, and more than 100,000 in six months. Judges were presented with white gloves signifying no cases to be tried. Alcoholism was halved. At times hundreds would stand to declare their surrender of Christ as Lord. Restitution was made; gamblers and others normally untouched by the ministry of the church came to Christ."[2]

The Welsh revival shows us what is possible when people experience the power of God's transformation. The world will not only notice but also experience a change itself when God's people begin to act like Jesus, when God's church lives like the body of Christ.

We believe that God is still calling the church to act and live on a mission with the same transformational power. We have hope—and we find it in the Scriptures. This hope is not like the hope of those outside God's covenant calling. Many times we think of hope in terms of possibility only. We say, "I hope that will happen." Or "I have high hopes." But this sort of hope suggests hopes can be dashed. In God's economy, our hope is sure. We have the promises of God before us in the Bible, and God never lies. Because of this, we don't have to "hope against hope" that God's gospel will be power, that His Word will not return void, or that He will be making all things new. He has promised these things, so we can cling fast to a solid hope, a hope that will not put us to shame. And as we have pored over the research presented in this book we have "high hopes" about churches that lay hold of the sure hope of God's promise to transform lives with the gospel.

Some may want to jump right into the research process, described in general in chapter 2 and in detail in the appendix. Others may want to jump into what we learned and the truths to apply, which start in chapter 3. But we thought a good place to start would be sharing how God is still faithful despite the challenges and discouragements in this ministry age.

God's Word First

The Word of God is always the best place to begin. God's Word always speaks with greater clarity and truth than anything we can muster up. That which has been inspired by the Holy Spirit thousands of years ago speaks to us today with startling immediacy. While we and our churches shift from fading to relevance, the Bible is always relevant, in every second of every century. One of the great promises it makes along these lines is that, though the church often looks and feels rough around the edges, God is always at work in His people.

In Zechariah 4, a ragtag remnant of Jews had moved back to Jerusalem. After being defeated and deported by Assyria, and then by Babylon, they returned to their homeland. We can only guess what little shreds of hope they carried in their weary hearts as they approached what was once the great city gates of Jerusalem. After seventy years of exile, most had only heard about, and only a few had witnessed, the grandeur of the great city. Undoubtedly, as they straggled into the destroyed city and surveyed the fallen walls, their hearts began to sink further. And when they finally surveyed the rubble that had once been the temple—the very place where God's literal presence was said to dwell—they had to have been utterly demoralized.

From Ancient to Modern Times

The analogy is not perfect, but many people today surveying the state of the North American church see similar destruction. As I (Ed) have written, some of those stats are overblown (see my article in January 2010 *Christianity Today*, "Chicken Little Was Wrong"), but there are some great concerns. Even if some of the stats are wrong, many Christians and churches *feel* as if they are in trouble. The result is practically a psychosomatic spiritual malaise. (In fact, one of the reasons we believe the negative statistics, even when they're not entirely accurate, is because they reflect what we believe.)

Everyone agrees we need some rebuilding. In the Old Testament, the remnant persevered through their distress and prepared to rebuild the house of God. But can we navigate our way through our own distresses and rebuild the hurting churches today?

We are praying that the insights gained from this study will lead many back to the mission from God. We pray God will use the discoveries made through this research for the revival of God's church. Learning from our ancient counterparts, the goal today must be a rebuilt church. The Jews eventually found hope in God's purpose. Churches with transformational practices are holding on to this hope as well.

We can look at many reasons why some North American churches today have ceased to become transformational. For some, it is simply a lack of focus. For others, it is external disruption or internal dissension. Some churches are too busy in maintenance mode. Some are too frantic in crisis mode.

We also see what many of you see in your churches—weary leaders. Some are physically tired from many long years in ministry. Some are emotionally tired from the rigors of routine pastoral ministry. Some are spiritually tired from the manipulation, dishonesty, and abuse of their congregations. Some are just tired of spinning their wheels, rapidly approaching the crushing realization that their church is plunging into spiritual impotence. We are encountering many defeated leaders who are just trying to survive. They have long lost the zeal to take the community by storm for Christ. These leaders are the burned and the burned out.

But the more things change, the more they stay the same. We see the same predicaments throughout history and find the principles for renewal and healing from the ancient words of Zechariah from the Spirit of our ageless God.

Zechariah heard from God and was used in God's plan for the Israelites returning to Jerusalem. As Zechariah began to see a series of visions from God, the fifth vision found in Zechariah 4 speaks to the message of the Transformational Church:

> The angel who was speaking with me then returned and roused
> me as one awakened out of sleep. He asked me, "What do you
> see?" I replied, "I see a solid gold lampstand there with a bowl
> on its top. It has seven lamps on it and seven channels for each of
> the lamps on its top. There are also two olive trees beside it, one
> on the right of the bowl and the other on its left." Then I asked
> the angel who was speaking with me, "What are these, my lord?"
> "Don't you know what they are?" replied the angel who was
> speaking with me. I said, "No, my lord." (vv. 1–5)

Transformation Begins with God

Zechariah the prophet and priest received a vision. Ultimately he would deliver it to Zerubbabel, the one to lead the rebuilding effort for the house of God. The first thing we see in this vision given by the angel of the Lord is a solid gold lampstand with a bowl on its top. Immediately the ancient hearer of this prophecy would understand that the solid gold lamp represented purity. But more than metallic purity is represented here.

Lamps, by design, emanate light. Even though Zechariah was slow to recognize the significance of the lampstand, asking "What are these?" (Zech. 4:4), the listeners receiving this word would recognize that this is a vision from God. How? The purity of gold and the emanating light represent God the Father.

There can be no renewal, revival, or rebuilding without a vision for and an experience of the all-consuming, all-illuminating presence of God.

Next we notice seven lamps on the lampstand and seven channels, which is where the oil flows to the lamp. This particular arrangement reveals oil flowing in seven different ways to produce seven different lights. If you are even somewhat familiar with biblical numerology, you probably know that the number seven in the Bible is the number of completeness, the number of per-fection, and the number of wholeness. If you know much about biblical symbolism, you probably know that throughout Scripture oil is symbolic of God the Holy Spirit. So between the emanating lampstand, the seven lamps, and the seven channels of oil, the vision being given here is one of God's presence.

There can be no renewal, revival, or rebuilding without a vision for and an experience of the all-consuming, all-illuminating presence of God.

If the Transformational Church initiative is not about God, His power, and His strength, then we don't want any part of it. Certainly this project is about research. Certainly it is about the reality taking place in North American churches. Yes, it is about the hundreds of hours of interviews by our consultants. And it is about the reams of data that came back from the objective research. It is about all those things and more. But those are tools the secular world can use too. What we want to be about first and foremost is whatever God is doing. The Transformational Church is His church for

His mission to reach the world with His message of redemption through Christ. Otherwise it has no value.

Paul wrote to the Roman church about transformation. In Romans 12:2, he said, "Do not be conformed to this age, but be transformed by the renewing of your mind, so that you may discern what is the good, pleasing, and perfect will of God." Here's the lesson—our closest allegiances shape us, whether we align with the world or God. When we submit to God, we are brought to an understanding of His perfect will. As Romans 12 continues, Paul described how the parts of the body of Christ work together for ministry and mission. As we act like the body of Christ, we will be the ambassadorial missionaries our communities desperately need and God sovereignly commands.

The heart of the gospel we carry into the world is transformation. The transformation brings freedom from sin, rigid legalism, and hopelessness. Look again at what Paul wrote to another early church, "Now the Lord is the Spirit; and where the Spirit of the Lord is, there is freedom. We all, with unveiled faces, are reflecting the glory of the Lord and are being transformed into the same image from glory to glory; this is from the Lord who is the Spirit" (2 Cor. 3:17–18). The churches we discovered are interested in changing lives for more than just the sake of helping people become better. There are plenty of self-help movements in the world, and the church doesn't even do that sort of thing particularly well. Certainly we don't do it as well as Tony Robbins or Oprah. But making well-adjusted and well-behaved unbelievers is not the aim of Christian mission. Deep in their hearts, TCs want to see the gospel help people reflect the very glory of God in our cities. They want to shine the light of Christ not to make shiny, happy people, but to multiply the number of light-shiners and thereby magnify the light of Christ more and more in every corner, community, and culture. The hope of a Transformational Church is for a complete change of individual lives and all of culture.

During this initiative, we discovered stories about what is taking place in churches all around our country. Transformational Church is not just another program or project. We have seen churches that are watching God's grace change lives and His glory affect cities. We trust that as we share these stories you will see God is in the movement as well.

Leaving Willpower Behind

The first lesson we learn from Zechariah's fifth vision is that God is present and ready to do a great work in the life of His people. Zechariah's initial response to this revelation is one of confusion (as it often is for Christians today). He says in verse 4, "What are these, my lord?" The angel of the Lord in verse 5 responds with incredulity: "Don't you know what they are?" Zechariah in honesty and perhaps a little embarrassment replies, "No, my lord."

The vision continues in verse 6: "So he answered me, 'This is the word of the LORD to Zerubbabel: "Not by strength or by might, but by My Spirit," says the LORD of Hosts.'"

Remember, the "me" at this point is Zechariah. But in an interesting shift of focus, the message given is for Zerubbabel. In other words, the message to Zechariah is "Wake up, get up, move up, and go speak to Zerubbabel!" The message of verse 6 is to tell Zerubbabel that he's been trying to lead in the rebuilding of the house of God by his own leadership skills, by his own resources, by his own intellect. And while all of those things are good gifts provided by God, *without God* they will come to nothing. He tells Zerubbabel that the work can only be done by the Spirit of the Lord of Hosts.

We learn an important truth from this exchange. Leaders must leave their willpower behind. God will supply all the strength needed for the task. This is exceedingly difficult, especially as God tends to move and work in ways that appear to us inefficient, slow, or just plain confusing. We reckon ourselves much better strategists and implementers. But anything built on the ingenuity and design of man will always and ultimately fail. Only what is built on the wisdom and command of the eternal God will last. That is kingdom work, and it is the work the church is called to put its back into.

We approach the work of Transformational Church with a humility that says it's not about us and/or our abilities. It is about God alone. When we (Ed and Thom) write a book, we pray for God to teach through it. When an assessment tool is designed from the discoveries of the Transformational Church initiative, we hope for God to give guidance through it.

There is indeed a lot of bad news out there. We've done the studies, written the articles, preached the messages, and written the books. But many are waiting for some messages of hope. We're here to tell you that as long as God is in it, there's always cause for great hope.

We both have had the privilege of leading several churches through transition periods—from decline to turn-around. Though I (Ed) lead a research team and enjoy the work of research, my greater joy comes from leading a local church beyond a state of despair over their stagnation. The first lesson these churches must (re)learn is to rely more on God's empowered mission than the personal preferences of the congregation. This is often a difficult journey for many North American believers to make. It challenges our comfort and convenience, and it frustrates our personal visions.

> Churches do not change until the pain of staying the same is greater than the pain of change.

In a transitional period, when facing the need to trade willpower for God's strength, churches encounter a moment of pain. I like to put it this way: "Churches do not change until the pain of staying the same is greater than the pain of change." It is heart-rending and difficult to admit that stubbornly holding on to our own willpower is actually supplying the pain of decline or lethargy in a church. However, I am pleased to report that when God's people are willing to face the stark reality that their willpower brings no hope, they are in the proper position to be empowered by God.

In the Transformational Church study, we have found hope—hope to stop running on a religious treadmill that leads nowhere. It comes when we drop the façade that we know best, can do our best, and will see our best.

The hope to see a revived church, growing disciples, and transformed communities is found in seeking God's best.

Believing Beyond the Obstacles

Zerubbabel had every earthly reason to focus on the obstacles. The angel told Zechariah to give the message to Zerubbabel: "What are you, great mountain? Before Zerubbabel you will become a plain. And he will bring out the capstone accompanied by shouts of: Grace, grace to it!" (Zech. 4:7).

A mountain is indeed a large obstacle. The mountain was a symbol of all the human reasons, like the surrounding nations and their lack of resources, Zerubbabel could not lead the Jews to rebuild the house of God. But listen to God's answer to the mountain: "Before Zerubbabel you will become a plain." The obstacle will be leveled out, and then people will start to get excited about it. "And he will bring out the capstone."

One thing Transformational Churches discover is that God is indeed bigger and more powerful than any obstacle or challenge. Of course, all Christians believe this in theory. But TCs press on in faith, crazily trusting that when God said mustard seed faith could move mountains, He really meant it. The leaders and members in TCs feel deep down in their bones that if God is for them, who can be against them? The churches we met during this study are thriving congregations that believe in God more than they worry about mountains. They realize the obstacles are there. They simply trust that God will remove them and replace them with His presence.

Too many churches attempt to gain hope and strength from the sentimentality of a bygone era of ministry success. But commemorating past victories is not victory. Quite often it is nothing more than smoke and mirrors meant to distract from defeat. There is nothing wrong with remembering what God has done in the past, but we must not live there. Just as the Jews returning from exile were ready to celebrate because of what God was preparing to do in their own day, the Transformational Churches we encountered are always ready to move forward with God and in His mission.

Pressing on to the End

These words conclude the fifth vision: "Then the word of the Lord came to me: "Zerubbabel's hands have laid the foundation of this house" (Zech. 4:8). So he did begin the rebuilding of the house of God. But he stopped. And now "his hands will complete it" (v. 8). But take a look at verse 9. Will people say what a great leader he is? Will people say what a great program he had? Will people say what a grand scheme he devised? Will the Israelites say, "Oh, Zerubbabel, what awesome hands you have!" No. "Then you will know that the LORD of Hosts has sent me to you" (Zech. 4:9). When God rebuilds His house, people will know undeniably that it is a work of God.

The prophecy through Zechariah to Zerubbabel and Israel was for a point in time, but the lesson is still applicable. We are not expecting God to work in the exact manner in your church that He worked in leading the Israelites. But, we do expect that He will be at work. The fifth vision given to Zechariah was to signal that they were not left as orphans from God. They were still His people through whom He would be worshipped and His name would be declared to the nations.

When we reach back into the "clean white pages" of the Old Testament, we find some not-so-familiar stories like the interaction between God, Zechariah, and Zerubbabel. And in a narrative like it, we once again find hope. Hope that God is present with His people and empowering them to point men and women from every tongue, tribe, and nation to His redemptive glory. For Zerubbabel, God was directing him to rebuild the temple by the divine power and favor that would be granted to him. As the church leaders of today, God is just as present with you. You are not building a physical temple, but Christ has promised His presence and the power of the Holy Spirit to engage in His mission.

The Transformational Church initiative has taken a lot of human effort. The research, the book, the leadership study, the church assessment tool, and the consultant training are just the beginning. Obviously, it takes hundreds of man-hours to do the work. But we are not looking to hand you another research project. Do we really need another spreadsheet? Another bar graph? No, what we want to pass on to you is a spark. A spark of hope, a spark of joy, a spark of a compelling message about God's work in the North American church today. We are convinced that you and your church, like the Transformational Churches we discovered, can become messengers of hope, just like in the days of Zechariah (or in the days of the apostles) because our God is a rebuilding God who is still at work and still on mission.

We will not shy away from the harsher truths about the state of the churches in North America. But sometimes the tendency is to focus so much on the negative that we essentially act as if God no longer exists. The church, the communities we serve, the nation in which we live, and the nations where we send our missionaries are desperately looking for hope. They're looking for transformed lives and transformational churches. Our prayer is that the message of Transformational Church will deliver guidance on how churches make disciples and transform their communities by the power of the gospel.

Our prayer is that the Transformational Church initiative will be all about God. We pray God anoints the process. We think it can renew hope in North America for God's transforming power displayed through the local church. If you closely examine the churches mentioned throughout this book, you will inevitably find flaws. We are not presenting them as ideals to be cloned. But you will also find a contagious heart for God and His mission. They are allowing God to move them beyond programs and into His harvest fields, and we hope you will allow God to use their stories to move you and your church as well.

The Church

In his book *Crazy Love*, Francis Chan addressed his passion for the local church with a simple but radically needed call. "I'm going back to Scripture," he writes, "and seeing what the church was in its simplest form and trying to re-create that in my own church. I'm not coming up with anything new. I'm calling people to go back to the way it was. I'm not bashing the church. I'm loving it."[3]

We, in the same way, love the local church. We love it more than we love statistics and studies. That's why so much of this book is guidance for local churches. We can create numbers and charts all day, but we think it is more important to let the data lead us to knowledge, to let the conversations with Transformational Churches give us direction, and to share that advice with you.

We have no better ideas than God's, but we also believe that His bride is underachieving in the world. Thus, we have dreamt about and set out to discover what it will take to make a church transformational. Our only hope from the Transformational Church initiative is to move the church more fully into God's mission of redemption. The greatest result is to hear that the gospel is being more widely told and people are turning their hearts to follow Christ.

We are saying to churches and their leaders, "God is not done with you yet." We are asking God to give us transformed churches. We are calling the people to live transformed lives.

Given the all-encompassing power of our Almighty God and His unfailing love for His church and His mission for the lost sheep, we are excited about what God plans to do with our churches.

Welcome to His world of Transformational Churches.

2
Change the Scorecard

I (ED) LIKE TO think of myself as handy with tools, unlike Thom who calls a carpenter to hang a picture. I have a ten-inch compound miter saw with a slide. Oh, yes, it's as serious as it sounds. I love to build, though my wife says I just love to have tools to think about building.

There is an old saying among carpenters, "Measure twice, cut once." If you've ever done any home improvement project, you know why. I've filled plenty of trash cans with pieces of trim that were cut one inch too short or too long. In construction, it is critical that you measure properly before moving forward. It's critical you have the right measurement before you start the work. The same is true in Christian ministry.

Throughout the Scriptures, the people of God are often referred to as a building. It's ironic: the Bible says people are a building, and yet we often treat the building as if it were as important as the people.

Measure twice, cut once.

In the New Testament, the church is referred to as "God's household" (Eph. 2:19). Paul went on to write in that passage to say "the whole building is being fitted together in Him and is growing into a holy sanctuary in the Lord, in whom you also are being built together for God's dwelling in the Spirit"

(Eph. 2:20–22). As the church, God is busy framing us together as His people and building His church as a missionary force for His kingdom.

A house of any kind, physical or spiritual, begins with a dream and then requires a blueprint. The dream we have for the church is the hope for transformation. As we have talked with church leaders for decades, it is a dream we all share. Seeing God's people built into transformational missionaries for His kingdom is perhaps the greatest dream for any church leader. But we must know what we are building first.

After the dream comes the blueprint. It is not enough to know that measuring matters. You must begin measuring as you build. A great blueprint has all of the necessary details to frame a solid house. It gives the builder insight into how each piece fits together and how each room supports the other. A great blueprint can guide the way to a structurally sound house. But a bad blueprint sends us in the wrong direction, leads to shoddy construction, and ends in destruction. Many American churches used bad blueprints and pay the price for it decades later. When working with a blueprint, a builder must be sure that the measurements are solid.

You need bricks and mortar to build a house: but if the material is your sole focus, you end up with what looks like a pile rather than a home. The materials are crucial to the building, of course, but the blueprint makes the whole plan.

The blueprint for us is the Transformational Loop. As we studied churches across North America, we saw a repeating pattern of elements and practices that created a framework. As we explain the Loop in the chapters to come, your church can use it as a solid blueprint for framing the right ministries and cultivating the right environments in your church. It will help you to start strong and give you a guide to constantly assess how the "building" is doing.

> **The blueprint for us is the Transformational Loop.**

In building, what you measure is perhaps most important. Have you ever seen a builder measure the nails to see if the lumber will fit to them? No, they measure the lumber. You don't measure a light switch and then plan the building around it. In construction, we have to measure the right things. The church is no different. Spending all of our time measuring the outlying issues of ministry means we will miss the core mission of God. TCs spend their time measuring the issues that bring transformation to lives and communities rather than measuring nails to fit in lumber.

Measurement matters. It matters when you are building and it matters when you are assessing. Whether you are framing a house or building a ministry, measuring matters. As you begin to assess your church and ministry, how you measure is important to properly understand if you are creating an impact in the community. Perhaps most important is what you measure.

Measuring the Church

The issue of measuring success in the church has become an issue of debate in recent years. We have both served as pastors and professors. From a ministerial perspective we wrestled with the desire to see the church grow numerically and in maturity at equal levels. From an academic perspective we endeavor to teach ministerial students the value assigned to each.

Ultimately we believe that measurements matter for the church. Rather than eliminate it (as some would call for), we think a change in the scorecard is needed. We believe one of the most important measurements is ensuring that men and women are being changed by the power of the gospel. In our tradition, that is followed by baptism—and that is another important metric. Ultimately it is what every church wants—more people redeemed and forgiven by grace through faith in God.

New believers are an essential metric for every church. But other issues must be important as well. As we entered into the Transformational Church initiative, our hope was to discover what a TC does that facilitates more people becoming Christ followers, more believers growing in their faith, and more churches making an impact on their communities.

The Old Scorecard

Few churches use any system of accountability today. Many North American Christians perceive church-wide accountability as intrusive and overbearing. But we can only expect what we inspect. If leaders don't take a close look into the life of the church and the lives of believers, they should not be surprised when there is nothing worth reporting.

The old scorecard of the church valued the external measures of the three Bs: bodies, budget, and buildings. The North American culture likes to count and so does its church. So we count the number of people attending, the number of dollars being used, and the number of square feet being inhabited for the purpose of the church. "The old scorecard keeps us church-absorbed. As long as we use it, we will continue to be inward-focused, program-driven, and church-based in our thinking and leadership."[1]

But we can only expect what we inspect.

The old scorecard is based on a brick-and-mortar mentality that reinforces the church as a specific time and place occurrence. It is time to rethink the scorecard. Better yet, it is time to rework it.

Reggie McNeal in his book *Missional Renaissance* states it this way:

> "When the church thinks it's the destination, it also confuses the scorecard. It thinks that if people are hovering around and in the church, the church is winning. The truth is, when that's the case, the church is really keeping people from where they want to go, from their real destination. The destination is life . . . Abundant life is lived out with loved ones, friends, and acquaintances in the marketplace, in the home, in the neighborhood, in the world."[2]

We want to see people move off of the campus and into the field.

We have always measured new believers, membership, and the attendance of primary gathering times. Counting the number of new believers is easy. Then we measure how many people are members of the church.

Finally, we measure how many people attend the primary gathering(s) of the church.

These three have served as the gold standard metrics for how the church is progressing. We are not against those, but we don't think they are enough. Certainly, without those measurements, most others do not have any meaning for the church. But we need more.

> *The people know to expect accountability as a normative part of their spiritual development.*

Churches that are seeing lives transformed hold themselves accountable for more. They hold a high emphasis on accountability. Transformational Churches are places where their values and actions are made clear and the people have embraced the need to live them out. With other churches accountability comes with a sense of dread. Not so with TCs. The people know to expect accountability as a normative part of their spiritual development. It is simply a facet to the discipleship process of individuals, the growth of the church, and the transformation of the community. They see it as biblical rather than a perfunctory function of the church.

The Transformational Church Research

Thus our task was one to see if healthy churches created a new scorecard. We wanted to discover the differences between churches that grow and thrive and those that stagnate and languish. So LifeWay Research began asking questions. We asked a lot of questions to a lot of people, both pastors and church members.

In the fall of 2008, we surveyed an initial five thousand of seven thousand Protestant churches to discover qualities of the top 10 percent based on select criteria. With any survey there are presuppositions. Our first-tier criterion was this: "Do you believe the Bible is the authoritative guide for faith and life?" That's a pretty foundational question and we wanted to be sure that pastors agreed if they were part of the research. Our study was based on churches that would all work out of the framework that Christ is the way to salvation. With the authority of Scripture as a baseline belief, we could advance our study knowing we were dealing with churches of like mind.

By the time the study was done, seven thousand churches were contacted and surveyed. We believe it's the largest survey ever done with this focus for churches, and we hope it will be transformative. We've really tried to do our homework and to do it well.

> **By the time the study was done, seven thousand churches were contacted and surveyed.**

In the spring and summer of 2009 we interviewed more than 250 leaders from among the top 10 percent of churches qualifying as Transformational Churches in our description, and we developed a preliminary transformational survey tool. The tool has been shortened and serves now as the assessment tool used by churches to better understand themselves and seek a more transformative disciple-making ministry.

The first criteria we used was that the church must have grown at least 10 percent in worship attendance when 2003 and 2008 are compared. So we're looking for churches that have experienced some growth, but most experienced more than that. The church must have had a minimum 2008 worship attendance of fifty. Now why fifty? Does that mean we don't like churches of forty-nine? Not at all. It simply means that churches below fifty in attendance can change drastically from year to year. So much so that it is nearly impossible to track and to create adequate statistical benchmarks. As an illustration, when one family joins, the church could grow by more than 10 percent and would be defined as a growing church. One family leaves and the same church becomes a declining church. So we placed size and growth benchmarks into the study in order to eliminate wide variances.

The second tier for qualifying in the study included the percentage of worship attendees involved in some small group, Sunday School class, or similar group. In this we are making a statement. Simply put, we believe churches that are transformational will have people in small community. It is an assumption we believe to be true. It is a qualification for a church to be transformational.

As we continued this robust, research-driven process, we secured permission and sent out dozens of LifeWay Research consultants across the country to personally interview the pastors of qualifying churches. Many of the church leaders were so humble that they thought it a waste of time for consultants to visit their church. Yet it was their churches that provided so much of the transformational principles.

How Did We Get Here?

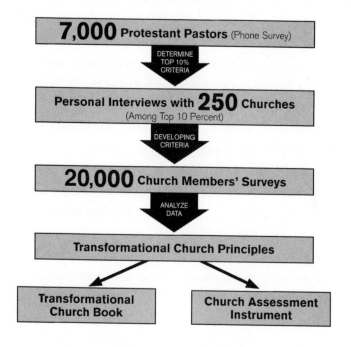

After the interviews were completed, we gathered the consultants for what became a wrestling match of ideas. Dividing them into small conversation groups, they compared notes and shared stories. Slowly but surely, certain values and activities rose to the surface of what they discovered. And on the flip charts scattered around a large room at LifeWay in Nashville, we began to see what they had recorded from the field—the values and practices of churches making a transformational impact in their communities. For two days Eric Geiger and I (Ed) sought to learn and discern what these consultants heard from the churches.

Through the research process we gathered both quantitative (numerical) and qualitative (human experience) data that allowed us to identify the principles that drive the Transformational Church initiative. Our observation was that the positive responses of agreement to the diagnostic questions were consistently and significantly stronger in TCs over the other churches in our study. We have included an appendix to this book that provides a more technical description of how the research was accomplished. We are certain it has been done with integrity and supports a clear path to help your church take the necessary steps toward being a transformational force.

We also have chosen to report the names of real churches. There is always a danger in that, but we prefer telling their stories. Some will object that Lutherans, Pentecostals, Methodists, and Baptists are all cited as places where God is at work. So be it. We see God at work in different kinds of churches and are glad to celebrate that here.

Also, we know that some of these churches may have (by the time this is published) changed for the negative, leaders may have stumbled, or the situation may have changed. Again, we know that transformation is, at times, fragile. We all fail and often fall. So, we have decided to do so anyway: use some names and share their stories. Why? Because in the stories we see God at work—and it encourages us and "provokes us to love and good deeds" (Heb. 10:24). That's worth the risk.

The New Scorecard

As evidenced in our research, outside assessments are growing in popularity in Transformational Churches. Assessments are not flawless. However, when based on sound research, they can reveal weaknesses and blind spots local churches will not normally see. The popular Web site YouTube provides an amazing illustration of this reality. In one video, two teams of people were featured, one wearing black and another wearing white. You are asked to count the number of times the five-person team in white passes the ball while they quickly do a figure eight type movement with the black team. The final number was thirteen. But then the question is changed after the count. You are asked, "Did you see the bear moonwalking in the video?" The video is replayed, and to the amazement of most people, a man dressed like a bear moonwalks right through the middle of the exercise.

The video is intended to illustrate how easy it is to be blind to something obvious if you are not looking for it. (Try it.) We all need internal and external assessment if our passion is to maximize our usefulness for God. God can use assessment processes to inspire change for local churches.

One of the issues the church wrestles with today (at least in North America) is what we measure and how we measure it. Understanding that it is a sensitive issue for all pastors and churches, we felt it necessary to measure what is always measured. But stopping with previous measurements did not seem to be wise given the discoveries of the TC study.

The ultimate measure of the church is to see people following Christ and living on mission. Redemption is always a central value for the church. We believe and recognize that more people becoming disciples is a key, but other objectives of the Christian life must be addressed and measured so we can see the strength of a church.

We are calling for a new scorecard.

The TC study revealed a statistical difference among the top 10 percent of churches and the other 90 percent. As we explain the categories and elements discovered from the research, one thing will be clear—it is not always a tidy list. But in a research-driven process, points are rarely neat and alliterated. Nevertheless, they can change our perspectives.

We are calling for a new scorecard. This scorecard would count what's important—people coming to Christ and living in Christian community— but also counts the other important issues as well. At its essence the new scorecard must measure how well we are making disciples. As you know, a disciple is more than a convert. A disciple begins as a convert but matures beyond his or her "new birth" date.

Disciples are those who trust Christ alone for salvation and follow God in a maturing process of faith and life. So our new scorecard will include the number of conversions but also includes other key aspects to the process by which a church facilitates the disciple's life.

The new scorecard measures the tangible. We were able to accomplish this in the TC surveys the same way churches do every week. We ask questions that are quantifiable, measurable by numbers. The scorecard measures the number of leaders being produced in a church. It measures attendance at worship, Bible study, and leadership training.

The new scorecard also measures the intangibles. Counting and intangible are two concepts that do not easily come together. In the TC surveys we found a relationship between certain issues and maturity in a church. But most issues in the church are difficult to quantify. They are stories, expectations, and the unscheduled occurrences of life. Yet often the intangibles are what make a church, well, a church. An issue like relational intentionality (chapter 5) cannot be measured easily with numbers. But its presence or absence is noticed. Its presence brings about health and growth. Its absence almost certainly delivers a death knell to a church.

The Transformational Loop: The New Scorecard

We made the decision early on that the research would drive our conclusions. We both have ideas as to what makes a strong disciple-making ministry. But the point of the Transformational Church initiative was not to justify our opinions or past research. We intentionally came into this process without a logo, framework, or set of principles we were determined to put in front of you. In other words, we were not looking for a neat set of rules for you to follow so everything will be smooth in your church. From years in the field of research, we know that presuppositions are impossible to eliminate, but a model built from them is normally too tidy and most likely faulty.

As we pressed forward through the research, we discovered these seven elements that fell into three categories. Obviously, the math does not work out in a balanced formula. But again, we were not looking for a formula. We were looking for spiritual practices rooted in the Scriptures that God used to deliver transformation. In TC we found the principles that transform people to look like Christ, congregations to act like the body of Christ, and communities to reflect the kingdom of God.

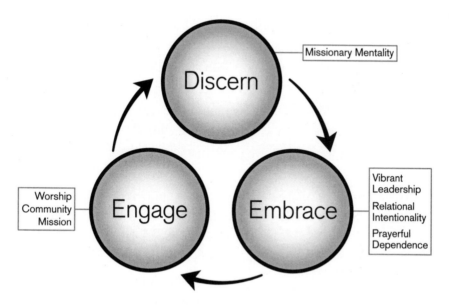

Transformational Loop

Perhaps an aside is needed here for clarity. Throughout the rest of the book, we will unpack each of these seven elements. There will not be a standard "Seven Steps to Success" for each principle or category. We hope to let the Scriptures do the work to illustrate how God is working in His church to proclaim the Christ and expand His kingdom. So be aware that you will need your thinking cap on and a pen handy to write in the margins and scribble notes to yourself.

The Transformational Loop is composed of three categories with seven elements. We discovered in each of these elements the churches that were measured to be transformational. Each element stands on its own as an idea but is dependent on the other elements in order to take effect in the church. Let's briefly explore each.

Discern

As we surveyed the best churches in our study, it became obvious that they are churches actively seeking to understand their community. But they do not stop with a list of facts and figures about it. The Census Bureau can tell you the raw data of your community, but churches seeking to be transformational take the work a step further. They move from number crunching to spiritual discernment.

Discerning your context begins with gathering information. A church must look around and see who lives around them. Rather than hoping for different people to move into the community, we are called to care for those who are already present. So we gather information about the community. But when we do, we are gathering information about real people, not just an anonymous mass.

TCs ask real questions about those in a community. Who lives here? What are their hurts? What are their dreams? Where do they spend their time? How do they relate to one another? They want to know about their neighbors.

> The churches we discovered with this transformational practice are serious about fulfilling Christ's command to "make disciples of all nations" (Matt. 28:19).

Once we have a grasp of the people in the community, then it is time to put discernment to work. Discernment moves the believer from observation to action. In what we uncovered, TCs use the information for a purpose. That purpose is to make disciples who are on a kingdom journey. Many churches know facts about their community but do little about those facts. Think of the difference that could be made if churches made the needs of the community the priority for their ministries and activities.

In the Discerning Your Context category, the element identified in TCs is Missionary Mentality. It is a singular element that summarizes the perspective and objective a church holds about the people around them. It is the sense that we are not here by accident but sent by God. The Missionary Mentality means that the church understands the community and will minister in contextually appropriate ways to reach local people with the gospel. The Missionary Mentality helps with the church's global vision as well. A church operating as a missionary in its local community is more likely to see the need for active participation in the global mission of God as well.

Discernment informs a church's values and activities. "Moving to an external focus pushes the church from doing missions as some second-mile project into being on mission as a way of life."[3] The churches we discovered with this transformational practice are serious about fulfilling Christ's command to "make disciples of all nations" (Matt. 28:19).

Embrace

Because we consistently fall into old and ineffective patterns of behavior, people need to be reminded of the why behind the what. Our actions need the right motives. Churches seeking transformational ministries embrace the right values.

The first element of Embrace is Vibrant Leadership. Leadership is a necessity in any environment where movement is needed. We found TCs to be places where positional leadership was less important. Positional leadership is when a person expects to be listened to and followed simply because of their title. The Vibrant Leadership seen in our top-tier churches did not have such a pedestrian understanding. The leaders in these churches showed passion for God, His mission, and its transforming power on people. They seek ways to move all believers into places of effective leadership for the mission. Those who followed these leaders often noted that the leaders led more by their examples and values rather than by dictates.

The second element of Embrace is Relational Intentionality. The church was designed by Christ as a collection of people participating in one another's lives. We see it as a critical step in

> *Transformational Churches are places where these important values are not just touted on a church Web site but are embraced by the congregation as a whole.*

the development of the church to help Christians deliberately connect with one another. Both accountability and encouragement occur as a church creates an environment where long-term relationships are held in high regard.

The third element of Embrace is Prayerful Dependence. When we entered the study, we knew that any truly transformational work is done only by God Himself. The churches we encountered believed that as well. But more than believing, they showed a natural disposition of communicating with God about the hope for transformation. We rarely encounter a church that denies the need to engage in prayer. Churches displaying transformational ministries revealed a dependence on prayer rather than a program for prayer. Their need to connect with God in prayer was evident and motivated by mission rather than selfish needs.

Transformational Churches are places where these important values are not just touted on a church Web site but are embraced by the congregation as a whole. These values serve as guideposts to move the churches from their context into action for their community.

Engage

The third category of the Transformational Loop is Engage. All churches are located somewhere, value certain principles, and have certain activities. But activity for activity's sake is of little value. In our study's top-tier churches, they engaged the right actions that led to transformation. The focused activity of these churches led to making disciples.

The first element of Engage is Worship. Everyone worships something. For some it is self, and for others it is an object of this world. Leading people to connect with the one true God who should alone be worshipped is the focus of transformational activity. The worship witnessed in TCs contains an element that stood out to our research team: expectancy. When people arrived for worship, they knew something great was going to happen. They trusted God to deliver transformation rather than musicians to deliver a good show.

The second element of Engage is Community. In referring to community, we do not mean the geographic location of the church. Rather, we mean the activity of joining lives together. These churches are serious enough about relational intentionality that they create systems to put people in community with one another. The people of transformational churches actively connect people to one another through ministry systems such as home Bible studies, small groups, Sunday School, and service groups.

Both believers and nonbelievers were encouraged to engage actively in community with one another. Though these churches held a sure view that God alone can transform a person, they have learned that it often occurs in the atmosphere of a small group of friends.

The third element of Engage is Mission. The reason behind much of the thinking, motivation, and activity of a TC is God's mission to make disciples of Christ and to engage the world as Jesus calls. They are diligently following God in order to see people transformed who will, in turn, transform the world. Evangelism is not taught as a periodic program but as a natural way of life. Joining together the elements of a missionary mindset and relational intentionality, churches led their people to understand disciple making as the normal state of the Christian's life. For them mission is always the priority.

> **The focused activity of these churches led to making disciples.**

Transformational Churches are not places with a set number of programs but places that know how to prioritize their activities. They have assessed their context in relation to their values, and it drives what they do. Rather than holding on to activities for tradition's sake, they act according to what is contextually appropriate to fulfill their values.

Principles of the Loop

As we progressed in our research, three framework principles came to light about the Transformational Loop: how a church connects to the loop, the cathartic experience, and convergence of elements.

Connecting to the Loop

First, there is not one starting point in which all churches must enter. Often you have read, seen, or heard proponents of a particular methodology declare that a church must start "here." Then they define the mystical starting point. Our research did not show such a point. If there was one particular place where all churches could transition from decline or plateau to transformational, we would be glad to share it. But we cannot find one in the research.

All three categories and all seven elements are necessary parts for a church to engage in transformational ministry. Your church can begin anywhere in the Loop. We found that many of the TCs began the process by starting with their strengths. If your church is strong in prayer, begin a new journey of effective ministry through prayer. Still, other churches desired to work on their weaknesses. If God convicts that your church is weak in its missionary mentality, then begin by learning discernment and employing it into your context. The point here is that you can begin with a strength or a weakness.

Your church can begin anywhere in the Loop.

To help you do so, LifeWay Research has prepared a church assessment tool (find out more about it by visiting www.transformationalchurch.com). This diagnostic tool was written from and refined through the research process, so that the leaders and members of your church can better understand how God is bringing transformation to your community and where your ministries are weak.

The Transformational Loop appears as a continuous cycle without a starting point. Let it be a comforting thought that God can use any element to propel your church into a new era of transformational ministry.

Cathartic Experience

Change is difficult. But as we have reported through other books and research projects, change is desperately needed in North American churches. In order for change to take place, an intervening event must occur. Many times it is through a cathartic experience.

A cathartic experience is a moment of decision or change that is beneficial and liberating. These experiences occur because the status quo is unsatisfying or even causing degeneration. The experience can occur because of conflict that must be resolved or a realization that no forward progress is being made. No matter the reason for it, the cathartic experience is the moment when a church decides that what they have and what they are doing is not enough.

A typical scenario could play out like this composite story: Bethany Lutheran Church saw significant growth in the late 1970s. The older members fondly remember those days and often talk about the wish for similar circumstances. But they have seen many visitors, members, and pastors come and go over the last thirty plus years. The current pastor has been on staff for four years and hopes to see the church once again bring widespread change to the community. After a series of unpleasant business meetings last year and a decline in membership, the church leaders gathered together for prayer and discussion over the state of the church. And then it happens—a cathartic experience.

After a passionate time of prayer at the start of the meeting, members of the leadership begin sharing their hope that the church could reach more teenagers for Christ. Excitement begins to build in the room as they sense the Spirit's guidance in understanding the community. Together they resolve that going about life and ministry the same or hoping for a return to the 1970s will not persuade any to come to salvation. So they make a decision. The decision is to see their church engage deeply into God's mission for the salvation of the people surrounding them every day.

> *A cathartic experience is a moment of decision or change that is beneficial and liberating.*

The congregation begins to hear a clearer passion from the pastor about God's mission for the church. Those in leadership positions of the church convey an excitement about what God can do in the church, through the church, and in the world with the church. Soon transformation has happened on individual and church-wide levels. Their hopes come true—students and their families are engaged with the gospel, and many place their faith in Christ.

The above story is representative of what many churches in our study experienced. They came to a breaking point; with discipleship undefined and God's mission unengaged, they sought change. Through our study of these churches, we intend to help you understand better how to identify the areas in need of change and some beginning steps to becoming a Transformational Church. But you must commit to seeking your own cathartic experience that will propel you into the Transformational Loop.

Convergence of Elements

A final principle of the Loop we discovered was the common convergence of elements. Whenever a large study is done—and this one certainly was large—attempting to give definitive analysis is difficult because you are dealing quantitatively with people who think qualitatively. Research attempts to put numbers to the human experience. What naturally occurs is the discovery that principles intermingle.

Though we love to see churches that are strong in the area of leadership, it would be tragic to discover they are weak in the area of worship. Churches that compartmentalize the elements outlined in the Loop are not transformational. By segmenting transformational elements from one another, they render the elements ineffective.

Churches with transformational disciple-making allow for a free convergence of the elements. For example, the activity of community is influenced by the other elements of the loop. Once again community is in the category of Engage—engaging the right actions. It is the activity of the church where people connect through a small-group system that matures believers and persuades unbelievers. But an effective small-group ministry needs vibrant leadership to operate. Leadership in the church needs prayerful dependence on God to be vibrant. When we are prayerfully dependent on God, He will open our eyes to the mission and help us discern our context. When the Spirit has worked in us to see the community as He does, then we will be compelled to be out on His mission of making new disciples. A great convergence happens when we seek transformative change.

To enter the Transformational Loop successfully, one must be prepared to allow the elements to flow together. If all a group of church members wishes to do is pray, who will do the work of evangelism? If a group only wants to participate in worship, how will community be built in the church? We must challenge believers to participate in all areas where God affects transformation in our lives by the gospel.

As a church leader, teach the elements of the Transformational Loop as distinct ideas and practices but not as independent from one another. Thriving believers will naturally enjoy the convergence of multiple transformative elements in their lives. Growing churches will find growth more natural when encouraging the elements to work as one. Communities will be more readily changed to reflect the kingdom of God when they witness Christians that are fully formed disciples.

> *To enter the Transformational Loop successfully, one must be prepared to allow the elements to flow together.*

Conclusion

Every church faces choices of what it will celebrate and what it will ignore. Essentially, we are choosing what to measure. Like good builders, we need to choose well. Churches need to decide to measure the things that matter to the kingdom of God. The Transformational Loop, born from some of the most broad-reaching research we've done, can serve your church as the blueprint needed to measure the right things, and measure the right things properly.

A revised scorecard is needed. Again, we turn to our friend McNeal, "So we have no option but to tackle the scorecard if we want everyone to be playing the same game. A shift in what counts and is counted does not happen automatically. It involves intentional and persistent effort and significant reeducation and modeling in your own life and ministry behaviors."[4]

The new scorecard calls for an honest assessment of both the old and the new in what churches measure. The number of new believers and attendance are still important, but factors such as vibrant leadership, relational intentionality, and prayerful dependence must also be measured as well.

Now we recognize that for some, this book will be too connected to the existing church. They will want something more avant-garde that throws off the old shackles and ideas. This book may seem to be focused on churches as they are rather than how they theoretically should be. And, we are OK with that.

> *Churches need to decide to measure the things that matter to the kingdom of God.*

Transformational Church is based on research of existing churches—ones that are seeing genuine transformation. Thus, we are looking at what IS, and what God is doing among what is. So, it has fewer buzzwords found in cutting-edge writing. But, it is about how God is working and how your "normal" church can be a Transformational Church—and be used of God in abnormal ways.

You see, we love the church. All the new words and new ideas are great, but they have to help advance the mission and the work of God's church. It must help us see the church with a fresh perspective.

The new scorecard must continue to prioritize the greatest need of humanity, women and men being changed by the power of Christ. Churches must continuously engage in the ministry of making new disciples. And, it is more than that—it is disciples changed by Jesus that change their church that changes the world. So here it is. The definition of a Transformational Church and one that we hope will be characteristic of all churches.

A Transformational Church is a congregation that joins God's mission of sharing the gospel and making disciples. Those disciples become more like Jesus, and the church thus acts as the body of Christ transforming their communities and the world for the kingdom of God.

We are praying that your church will choose to go on the Transformational Church journey. We think you will find the information and inspiration needed to have your cathartic moment.

The cathartic moment is an "ABC" moment. You must have an (A) awareness that something needs to change in your church. You must then have (B) belief that God will transform your church. Finally, you must be willing to deal with the (C) crisis that comes from such change.

But we are getting ahead of ourselves. Let's first return to the Transformational Loop. Though it has no predetermined beginning point, the Missionary Mentality is a great place to begin.

To that transformational element we now turn.

3
Missionary Mentality

To the weak I became weak, in order to win the weak.
I have become all things to all people, so that I may by
all means save some. Now I do all this because of the
gospel, that I may become a partner in its benefits.
(1 Corinthians 9:22–23)

BY THE NUMBERS

The activities of our church are designed
to relate to the type of people who live in
our city or community. (64 percent strongly
or moderately agree)

Story of Success

Racially Reconciled . . . Generationally Rich . . . Thriving in the Heart of the City is how First Christian Assembly of God in Cincinnati, Ohio, describes their vision. Pastor Chris Beard and the historic Cincinnati congregation are in love with the Queen City and her people. The burden they carry is for the hurts, needs, and issues presented by city life. First Christian Assembly (FCA) believes God has planted them in a specific place to make a difference. They are committed to seek out the real needs in the city, join with like-minded churches, and go after those needs. By doing so Pastor Beard said they are able to make "the church visible to the city."

God gave Pastor Beard a burden that the church should reflect more of the ethnic composition of the community. Pastor Beard took the role of senior pastor around the time of extreme racial turmoil in Cincinnati. A nineteen-year-old African-American, Timothy Thomas was shot by a white policeman in 2001. The worst rioting in the history of the city took place for three days. At the time FCA church was 98 percent Anglo. Pastor Beard believes that one of the "key apologetics for the gospel" is found in Jesus' prayer in John 17 that His followers would be united.

A clear strategy was implemented with the vision of becoming "racially reconciled." Action steps included: communicate, teach supporting Scripture, diversify staffing, diversify board leadership, conduct classes about African-American history, conduct classes on other cross-cultural realities, and teach people how to fellowship together. What have been the results? Nine years later the church is now 65 percent white, 20 percent African-American, and 15 percent international. Recently the church celebrated the baptism of a young African-American woman named Brandi. She was the sister of the late Timothy Thomas. Thomas's brother, Terry, and his three children now also attend FCA. Transformational Churches engage the mission of God in their surrounding neighborhoods with a commitment to the church's immediate context.

TRANSFORMATIONAL LEADERS SPEAK . . .

"As God sent the Son into the world, so we are at core a sent or simply a missionary people. . . . This 'sending' is embodied and lived out in the missional impulse. This is in essence an outwardly bound movement from one community or individual to another. It is the outward thrust rooted in God's mission that compels the church to reach a lost world. Therefore, a genuine missional impulse is a sending rather than an attractional one."[1] —Alan Hirsh, *Forgotten Ways: Reactivating the Missional Church*

Discovering a Missionary Mentality in Transformational Churches

Understanding context, or a missionary mentality, is a key component in Transformational Churches. Transformational Churches live out the essence of disciple-making in their activities through worship, community, and mission. But they do so in the context of their culture. Worship occurs with an understanding of context. Mission into the surrounding neighborhoods occurs with an understanding of the church's immediate context. Likewise Transformational Churches express their values in light of their context. Leaders demonstrate a heart for the culture. Engagement into the community is done with relational intention, and the churches pray for their community. Simply put, Transformational Churches know, understand, and are deeply in love with their cities, communities, and people.

Where Are You?

Your ministry assignment has delivered you to a place. What does God want you to do? That is the wrong question, or maybe premature question. It may be a given that God has prepared, wired, and instructed you to plant a new or grow an existing church. The common mistake however is that the *how* can get fully developed in your head before you know the *who* and the *where*.

The ABC television drama *Lost* enjoyed popular and critical success. Millions have viewed the series since 2004. The story line was a hybrid of *Gilligan's Island*, *Survivor*, and *The X-Files*. A large passenger plane returning from Sydney, Australia, to Los Angeles crashes in the South Pacific leaving all surviving passengers stranded. The slow and mystical journey included flashbacks into the surviving passengers' lives as well as mysterious happenings on the island. The passengers learned a new reality day by day. No matter what they were thinking, their new

> *The common mistake however is that the how can get fully developed in your head before you know the who and the where.*

reality derailed everything. Their previous plans no longer mattered. The challenges of the island were dramatic and life threatening. The learning curve was high. Flexibility and adaptability were critical to effectiveness.

One thing that is true to life about the dramatic series is everyone has a story, a really big story. Their story is driving their every move. Just like real life all the people in the series have stories.

> *A critical mindset shift toward a more missionary mentality is from the idea that people **have** stories to people **are** stories.*

A critical mindset shift toward a more missionary mentality is from the idea that people *have* stories to people *are* stories. If people matter to God, how much more do their stories matter? If their stories matter, how can those stories help us help them? Our study revealed a lot of churches understood and practiced the *what* to various degrees. Worship (gathering), groups (growing together in smaller communities), and mission (engaging people outside their church) are a part of most churches. Even the *how* finds commonality across denominational, generational, and geographic lines (leadership, prayer, relationships). But the element of *where* creates a huge distinction for the Transformational Church. The context of ministry informs how it is carried out.

We must know the stories in our place of ministry. New episodes constantly present themselves. But as with the series *Lost*, to understand the new episode, you need to know what happened in the last. In fact, to understand the current episode, you are best served by knowing where it all started. To do worship, small groups, mission, leadership, prayer, and relationships effectively, you have to know the story of the people to whom God has sent you.

> *We must know the stories in our place of ministry.*

If you are passionate about the people and community where God has sent you, and if you love them as He does, you will be motivated to know and understand their story. Sadly, Christian leaders are often more in love with the way they do church than they are in love with people in their community.

Missionaries see people as unique and valuable. Jesus saw people as individuals and in groups. The crowds were important to Jesus because of the people in them. Crowds are not trophies to be won. Neither are the crowds "projects" to be completed. Influencing masses of people is not for the leader's affirmation or self-worth. Crowds are important because of the incredible worth of people.

The psalmist provides insight into the value of the people to whom God has called you. "I will praise You, because I have been remarkably

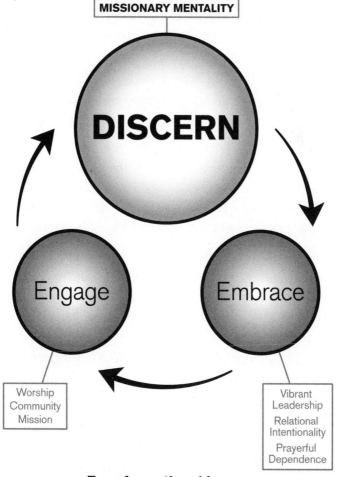

MISSIONARY MENTALITY

DISCERN

Engage

Embrace

Worship
Community
Mission

Vibrant
Leadership

Relational
Intentionality

Prayerful
Dependence

Transformational Loop

and wonderfully made. Your works are wonderful, and I know [this] very well" (Ps. 139:14). If people are valuable, then they are worth getting to know. Hearing and understanding their stories will be the key to introducing them to Jesus Christ.

TC Heart for Mission

As we surveyed the Transformational Churches, it became obvious that they had a keen sense of their community. In surveying the pastors and people of these churches, we asked for a response to this statement: "The needs of our city or local community inform our local missions strategy." A majority (53 percent) strongly or moderately agreed with the statement. Now on its own that is not enough to think a church is being driven by a missionary mentality. But in pushing the issue, we discovered that churches with a TC heart made their context vital in all their decision making.

Sadly, Christian leaders are often more in love with the way they do church than they are in love with people in their community.

When TC members were asked about their passion for the community, not every member took a strong position. Yet significantly, more members strongly agreed than members of non-TCs. Take a look at the following:

- "Our congregation cares deeply about the people in our city or community." (81 percent strongly or moderately agree)
- "Our church leaders think as missionaries in how they view the cultural context within our region." (67 percent strongly or moderately agree)
- "Our church members are frequently reminded about the unique opportunities to impact those who live in the city or community surrounding the church." (69 percent strongly or moderately agree)

But, also important, their community indicated a positive sense of the churches that showed this type of commitment to the community.

is often part of God's process that leads to more people and places to minister. To help this process TC leaders must know who they are, who the church is currently, and how to connect the body of Christ to the community at large.

I (Ed) have invested a lot of my life either planting churches or helping planters plant churches. Often church planters go through an initial phase of restlessness that God uses to speak to them about His new assignment. The restless phase is followed by a search for those who have succeeded at doing what the planter feels he may be called to do. It is the research

> *TCs are restless to look, learn, and live out the gospel.*

phase. Personal conversations are not the only part of this phase. Reading, conference attendance, and Web surfing can begin to paint a picture of what a church plant needs to look like. I've seen that many church planters plant churches in their heads and not their communities. But TC leaders and believers don't allow that to happen. They decide to plant (or in most readers' case, pastor) in the community. They activate ministries that are on behalf of the people to whom God has called them.

What phase is missing when a church is planted in the mind and not in the community? What is missing when a church decides how ministry will be done without regard to the mission field surrounding their church campus? The missing phase is prayer and discovery.

The people who live there should have a say in what God's planting project will look like. This is not to suggest they have a vote. But if the church is really to reach them, then how they are best influenced for Jesus is a big deal. Remember, He calls you to a people first and then to the task.

Three Default Modes

The missionary mentality results in transformation. Without the strong sense of call to a people, where does a leader get his agenda? Actually, there are three common default modes for a leader without a calling to a people to get his agenda. We often see leaders becoming one of these three things to fill the void left by not having a geographic people group calling.

A Deconstructionist

The church today is going through an era of turmoil, lack of results, and frustration for many. This has produced a discontented tribe of leaders who obsess with what they will not do anymore. They are the deconstructionists and are often driven by anger rather than love or hope. They are angry at the existing church that does not get it and the previous generations who care more about preserving tradition than reaching the lost.

People in established churches view deconstructionists as arrogant mavericks with no regard for doctrine and a willingness to resort to any method to grow churches. Many of these new, entrepreneurial leaders have been hurt and have caused hurt in existing churches.

The sins of the deconstructionist are an overreaction to the real enemy and an overstatement of the hopelessness of the existing church. The deconstructionist takes great pride in pointing out fault but can also get lost in that world. They are often consumed with proving their point. But "We'll show them!" has never been a biblical or an effective mission statement.

The answer is to engage all leaders with a discerning mindset about God's unique plan for delivering ministry into distinct communities. God has a diverse army of followers to reach a diverse and lost mission field. Some leaders are more wired to lead entrepreneurial efforts in starting new churches. Two words are critical for leaders in existing churches and their response to entrepreneurial church planters: "bless" and "release"! New churches are proven effective in reaching more people with the gospel of Jesus Christ.

Other leaders are more effective at taking existing structures and people to lead into the harvest. Two words are critical for leaders in new churches and their responses to existing leaders: "affirm" and "embrace"! Existing churches are great tools in the hand of God for local communities and the world. They have the resources and track record to make a difference. TCs collaborate with diverse gospel-centered leaders to do missionary work in their community.

A Methodologist

Methodologists are obsessed with what they will do better than the rest. Our approach to God's work is important. Methods matter! Certain methods for reaching people may be effective during a certain era or in a particular geographic location. Unique and gifted people may be able to maximize an approach to getting results that will not have the same results for you.

> **Tools do not work, people do!**

Methods are tools. Tools have a purpose, but their purpose is not about them. You may value your tools, but a tool does not possess commitment and hard work. Don't believe the overpromise of a tool that is guaranteed to make your yard beautiful. Tools do not work, people do! Have you ever nominated your rake for "rake of the year" in your home owners' association? If you win first prize in your neighborhood beautification contest, will anyone ask to see your lawn mower? No one will attribute your award to the inanimate tools in your garage. Sometimes our genuine desire for results causes us to grasp for anything. There is one purpose for your tools—to help you get results. The same goes for the methods you choose. What gets results in your front yard goes beyond the tools. Hard work and commitment are critical factors. A tool does not work by itself.

Methods are also like bread. Hot, fresh bread with a little butter and homemade jam—there is nothing like it. The smell is potent enough to make you gain weight. Then you confront the challenge of limiting the amount you eat. Hot, fresh bread is most attractive for a moment in time but will soon become moldy. For a moment in time that specific loaf of hot bread was perfect. Methodologists approach ministry dreams with great ideas and choices. But like yesterday's bread, the shelf life of a method normally does not endure long term. Missionaries know when to throw away the bread that was effective for a season. But now they must move on because they care more about people than methods. Timing matters when choosing methods.

Finally, methods are like musical instruments. The real effectiveness of certain methods is directly connected to the skill and passion of the person who uses them. New Orleans' Louis "Satchmo" Armstrong is considered the greatest jazz trumpet and cornet player in history because of his excellent skills with ordinary musical instruments. None of us would grab a trumpet and attempt to play like Satchmo. Not only was Louie Armstrong a disciplined musician; he was naturally gifted. Methodologists assume that the secret is the choice of instrument. Yet the person, the timing, and the dedication are all factors that result in the sweet music of life change.

> *Transporting methods devalues the people in your community.*

The sin of the methodologists is method worship. God gets no glory through our music style; He gets glory in the way we sing the style we have chosen. God gets no glory in our evangelism program choice. He gets glory in our passion to have gospel conversations with people far from Him. What ultimately matters is what God has placed in the heart of the missionary leader and church. The leader should hold or guard no method but be free to choose, create, and embrace what is biblical and what works.

An Impressionist

Impressionists are students of conferences and successful leaders. Obsessed with who they will do ministry like, impressionists ignore critical context factors that make successful leaders do what they do. Successful leaders can bring great value to everyday leaders who want to be successful for God. However, irresponsible leaders emulate a ministry hero and transport that person's methods into their own community without proper discernment. Every community in North America feels unique because it is unique. Transporting methods devalues the people in your community. What a church leader does in Chicago cannot necessarily be repeated in Dallas simply because a leader likes the leader and the method.

Ghosting is a prank described as "personal space invading." The idea is to copy another person's movements as close and as long as possible without the person noticing. It is entertaining to watch but unhelpful in church leadership. Impressionists are guilty of getting way too close to the way successful leaders operate. They can preach their sermons word for word. They can even dress like them with the sincere hope of producing the same results. Learning from the way successful people approach God's work can be of great value. Practicing certain methods can work. But impressionists are missing the adventure of learning who lives in their mission field and finding ways God can open those hearts to the gospel.

Contextual Ministry in Transformational Churches

- "Our church leadership understands the cultural context surrounding our church." (77 percent strongly or moderately agree)

Transformational Churches had an interesting insight into their leaders. At a rate of 77 percent, church members in TCs strongly agreed that their church leaders understood the context surrounding their church. But the implications are wider than that. Look at the next statistic.

- "Everything we do is in the language and culture of the people we are trying to reach." (58 percent strongly or moderately agree)

TCs are the places where the missional believer feels at home. Better yet, they feel as if they are being sent out effectively.

But we now come to a difficult issue. Rather than our extracting best practices of contextual ministry from Transformational Churches for you, we think it better to read the examples of the missionary mindset of transformational churches. As we look at churches who embrace the transformational practice of contextualization, consider this question: What does it look

What does it look like for a church to be contextual in the community where God has sent them?

like for a church to be contextual in the community where God has sent them?

Pastor Chuck Williams, Live Oak Community Church, Lubbock, Texas– "We talk a lot about our thumbprint, . . . and for us the key element is authenticity. That's a big value in West Texas. You know, they want real. I would say there is a cultural component to wherever you are. To embrace the values of that culture that are wholesome and good and be the church where people and love occur."

Chuck talked about the importance of door-to-door survey work to discover what the people of Lubbock were thinking. Initially people were reluctant to admit they did not go to church. Once able to get past the reluctance, it was learned that people really wanted authenticity. Many of them felt the church wanted their money. The contextual challenge became how to stay financially viable, teach biblical stewardship, and not get caught up arguing about money. Pastor Chuck also discovered that many they surveyed thought they already knew what was going on at church even though they were not involved in a church.

The result was that church leaders at Live Oak believe "it's a sin to bore people." They attempt to avoid change for the sake of change. But Live Oak's understanding of people in their context has resulted in embracing practices that will help meet the needs of their specific region. For example, well-planned Sunday services are critical. Hearing from God as part of the planning process is how Live Oak and Pastor Williams define "well planned." Their values include authenticity, relevancy, creativity, and unpredictability. The values are lived out in practices.

Although similar conclusions could have been discovered in many historically churched communities, there is something to learn here. The people of Live Oak discovered the specific needs in their own community in real time. They did not necessarily depend on a book or conference to inform them of the "hot" methods. People in the church will display a much deeper embrace of what they discover in their communities than imported methods. Information delivered from books and so-called experts from other communities does not have the same influence.

Dr. Kenneth Keene, Trinity Assembly of God, Columbus, Ohio–The vision for reaching people through Trinity Assembly is anchored in the unique context of their church. "We cast the vision that we are going to push back darkness on the west side of Columbus," said Dr. Kenneth Keene. They are located in a blighted urban area of Columbus. Even city leaders assumed that Trinity Assembly of God would move out of their difficult location into the safer suburbs. Dr. Keene believes there are plenty of churches in the suburbs, and yet there are thousands of people to reach in the area where his church is located. Pastor and congregation feel a strong sense of call to the people in their area and minister with a heart for them. "We are going to push back darkness one soul at a time on the west side of Columbus," said Dr. Keene.

Pastor Thomas Sica, Open Door Baptist Church, Scranton, Pennsylvania— Pastor Thomas Sica discovered that religious perception is a major issue in his context. "Our area is heavily Catholic. In this area if it's not Catholic, it's a cult. If it's Protestantism, it's a cult." Many people use their Catholicism as a defense mechanism against being open to the gospel, according to Pastor Sica. He considers a first step of influence is to get them into their building for something other than a church service. Their location has been particularly conducive for a manger scene for Christmas. Open Door also hosts a Fall Fellowship with plenty of fun for families with the goal just to "get people on the grounds so they can walk through the building." The experiences of connecting make people less "terrified" when they are invited to a worship service.

Pastor Doug Levesque, Immanuel Baptist Church, Corunna, Michigan— According to *The Wall Street Journal*, Shiawassee County (pop. 70,000) ranked fifth in the nation in the number of young married couples needing preschool day care. Pastor Doug Levesque and Immanuel Baptist were determined to address the need. The Corunna community needed extra education. Local schools were out of money. Two elementary schools were in the process of closing. Immanuel realized their main demographic was young married couples with preschool children. Meeting the need was approached as a community service. Nothing unusual was required from the parents such as church membership to take advantage of their preschool. Special school programs included a presentation of the gospel. Immanuel also noticed the need for city sports leagues. They responded by the creation of the ISL, or Immanuel Sports League. Ministry strategy was driven by the greatest needs in their area. New relationships with people far from God were the results.

Changing the World, Not My World

Transformational Churches demonstrate a passion to touch the world. The exceptional part of TCs is that they are actively involved in praying, giving, and going to specific places to live out their passion. Why would this be exceptional? For some reason the talk among those who are Christian has become bigger but the action has become smaller. Often we rally around the compelling vision to change the world. The larger vision is more inspirational than the idea of making a bigger or better local church.

> *Transformational Churches demonstrate a passion to touch the world.*

Yet the cost of going combined with the overwhelming need makes worldwide action a more difficult scorecard. Where is the instant gratification in going to India? India is the second largest country in the world with a population of 1.2 billion people. India has thirty-five cities of more than one million people and three cities of more than ten million people. The population is 2.3 percent Christian and 80 percent Hindu. If the vision is to change the world, India is included. Through e-mail, Skype, Facebook, and Twitter, the world has become a smaller place. We can connect any place at little or no personal cost. Big is the new small. So it is easier to feel a greater connectedness and become content although we have little or no influence on the world at large.

Recently a pastor who called himself "missional" stated that his church needed to pull back on their global mission support to help people be missionaries in their own community. The idea of God with a world upon

His heart goes back to before the foundation of the world. The picture of a mighty God who loves every tongue, tribe, and nation is compelling. The reality is much greater than the picture. God's heart for the world becomes a mandate for His followers to love the peoples of the world and make disciples of every people group (Matt. 28:19–20). God's love for the world is more than a special offering, a mission trip, or a video clip. When we decide to embrace the mission of God, we embrace all 6.8 billion people. Transformational Churches have learned to address the need to work both locally and globally.

We believe that a missionary mentality matters . . . but any real missionary mentality must be global in focus. And, we believe that churches who want to be transformational and missional need to be careful to not lose a global focus. As the missional conversation continues and deepens, some seem to have lost that. And, we wonder what has occurred that has led to our blindness to the lost world around us? As we have listened to churches and leaders, we think there are several reasons. We think it is important to consider the reasons that some churches focus on transformation but forget global mission involvement and cross-cultural evangelism.

The first reason many missional Christians are uninvolved in God's mission is that some people have only discovered its personal dimensions. This is not to say they have somehow localized mission into their private life; that would make little sense. Rather, the encouragement for each person to be on mission (to be "missional") has trended toward a personal obligation to personal settings, rather than toward a global obligation to advance God's kingdom among all the nations.

"Missional" has experienced an unintentional merger with the false premise of a privatized Christianity. Being missional has degenerated (in some circles) to serve as the reason for personal projects carried out in personal spheres. Now, service toward personal projects in a personal sphere is not necessarily bad. But when the missional impulse is not expanded to include God's global mission, it results in believers moved only to minister in their own Jerusalems with no mind toward their Judeas, Samarias, or the uttermost parts of the earth (Acts 1:8).

A view of God's mission as a personalized mission can reduce it to geographical boundaries. People think of Acts 1:8 as a geographical progression instead of a historic illustration of God's mission and heart. Acts 1:8 was a real-time prophetic message foretelling the progression of the gospel. Jerusalem was not "their Jerusalem" (the original hearers of Acts 1:8) any more than you have a Jerusalem. In other words, Jerusalem was not symbolic of our personal domain. Jerusalem is the location of a once only spiritual-historical event: Pentecost.

The best modern metaphor for your Jerusalem is the place where you receive the outpouring of God's supernatural power through His Holy Spirit (salvation). Or your Jerusalem might be the place of a meeting with God where He expands your life mission. Your Jerusalem may be an unforgettable, life-altering God encounter. The implication for Acts 1:8 for missions is the "from everywhere to everywhere" responsibility of every Great Commission Christian on the planet. Filipino missionaries to the United States are living out Acts 1:8. Canadian missionaries to Ireland are living out Acts 1:8. African missionaries to Romania are also living out Acts 1:8. And of course, North American missionaries to Japan are living out Acts 1:8.

A privatized mission also drives people to work almost exclusively within their own people group. The gospel was sent through tongues to a multiethnic, multicultural church. In fact, there were no North Americans at Pentecost! We received the gospel cross-culturally. The word *nations* is not a political designation in Scripture but is used to describe people groups, particularly those people groups where the gospel has not yet gone. We have given ourselves greater permission (maybe to a fault) to speak of indigenous missions. Like it or not, your burden to reach the French is to be just as great as your burden to reach your indigenous tribe. It is easy to back away from difficult groups to more comfortable groups. Then our groups look less like God (multiethnic, multicultural) and more like us (tribal, prejudice).

So how did cross-cultural disciple making occur at Pentecost? God intervened. The supernatural power of God makes us effective witnesses for Him to the peoples of the world. Global Christians put their hope in joining His worldwide mission. God gets less glory when every Christian talks, thinks, dresses, eats, and lives alike. That looks more like a dysfunctional cult than a real movement that brings glory to God. God gets glory when people who dress, eat, talk, and live differently join around the table for a meal with one heart. After they have an authentic encounter with God, people who would not normally be caught dead in a room together greet one another with a holy kiss and call one another brother and sister.

> God gets glory when people who dress, eat, talk, and live differently join around the table for a meal with one heart.

In addition to reducing the mission of God to my own personal sphere, self-absorbed believers have learned another response. The response is, "I will only serve God in the area of my perceived gifts and passions." When the trend of "working in my giftedness" becomes an excuse for not working, then we have abandoned God's mission. We must not fear Jesus' invitation to come, take up one's cross, and follow Him—even when we must serve outside of our proverbial comfort zone. All of life is an opportunity to "mortify the flesh" and deliver the gospel. Transformational Churches find a way to launch people into significant local and global mission efforts using their strengths as they are empowered by the Spirit.

The second reason so many missional Christians are uninvolved in God's mission is some people have wanted to be more mission shaped and have made everything "mission." Missions historian Stephen Neill, responding to a similar surge in mission interest (the *missio dei* movement of the 1950s and following), explained it this way: "If everything is mission, then nothing is mission."[2] Neill's fear was that the focus would shift from global evangelization (often called "missions") to societal transformation (often called "mission"). He was right.

One reason for the shift in North America is due to the sea of statistics supporting the fact that we had truly become a predominately lost nation. North Americans have never been more spiritual and less Christian. The North American people have made their religious choices. New religious decisions are at best ambiguously biblical and Christian. Syncretism rules. However, syncretism is a clear choice against biblical Christianity.

Leonard Sweet was one of the first to promote North America as the largest English-speaking mission field in the world. He described the two "mission constituencies" as the "unchurched" and the "overchurched." Sweet described our challenge on the North American mission field this way:

> Only two countries have more nonbelievers than the US: India and China. The US is the third-largest mission field in the world. Unfortunately, our efforts at evangelizing the unchurched have all the pace of a southern summer. Few believers have relationships, much less friendships with non-believers.[3]

> **Growth for the church and growth of the individual believer occur when we move "out" by participating in God's mission.**

If the current realities of lostness in North America have caused confusion among North American Christians, the slide did not begin recently. Perhaps the decline began when we saw missions as something different, when North America was more "Christian." Historically, missions was something other people did in other places. We prayed for, supported, and pitied the tribes of Africa. We designated others to be their missionaries. We were not missionaries.

When asked about their willingness to step out into the work of the community, Transformational Churches were ready. Our survey found strong agreement among TCs to the following statement:

- "Our church is innovative and entrepreneurial in serving non-Christians outside of the church." (56 percent strongly or moderately agree)

Within the basic thinking of a TC leader and member is the desire to break out of the programs designed to keep people "in." Growth for the church and growth of the individual believer occur when we move "out" by participating in God's mission, not by simply labeling everything as mission.

One North American church's Web site recently identified their ministry as missional, which they proceeded to define as "reaching out to the community to invite them to come." See what is happening in the church? Another's young adult community service project consisted of landscaping the church grounds. Inviting people to church and cleaning up the church are noble endeavors, but that's not what being missional is all about. It demonstrates the fuzziness that creeps in when labels become catchalls. And as the outer edges of the missional label get fuzzy, so does mission to the outer edges of the world.

Jesus presented His disciples with a prediction of the future behavior of authentic Christians: "But you will receive power when the Holy Spirit has come upon you, and you will be My witnesses in Jerusalem, in all Judea and Samaria, and to the ends of the earth" (Acts 1:8). Notice that the context changed but the behavior did not. What we are to do for Jesus in Nashville, Seattle, or Miami is the same thing we are to do in Cuba, Uganda, or Taiwan. Nothing changes but the location. Future Christians would be accountable to witness to the story of Jesus everywhere according to Acts 1:8. To say the vision was big is one thing, but the reality is the vision was ridiculous in human terms. Yet we are to inherit the mission of God and carefully apply it to our lives and ministry.

The third reason so many missional Christians are uninvolved in God's mission is that many are focusing on being good news rather than telling good news. St. Francis allegedly said, "Preach the gospel at all times; when necessary, use words." Interestingly enough, Francis never actually said this, nor would he have done so. He was in a preaching order. But it is a pithy quote tossed into mission statements and vision sermons in churches around the country. Why? It seems that many place a higher value on serving the global hurting rather than evangelizing the global lost. Or perhaps it is just easier. We do not wish to urge a dichotomy here but simply to note that one already exists. It is ironic, though, that as many missional Christians have sought to embody the gospel, some have chosen to forsake one member of Christ's body: the mouth.

> We don't own mission, and it is not ours to define.

Proclamation versus justice has been falsely erected in the church's view of mission. The message increasingly includes the hurting but less frequently includes the global lost. One only needs to watch the videos to see the emphases: global orphan projects, eradicating AIDS, Christmas shoe boxes, and so forth. All of these causes now have advocacy groups, and rightly so, as they are important. However, their vocabulary and frames of reference do not frequently make room for evangelizing the people they touch. Missional churches seem to speak more of unserved peoples rather than unreached peoples. As we engage to deliver justice, we must also deliver the gospel regardless of anyone's status in a culture. TCs have found a place of convergence for both the message of the gospel and the ministries that should accompany it.

The fourth reason so many missional Christians are uninvolved in God's mission is many lose the context of the church's global mission and needed global presence. For whatever reason—the admirable one of commitment to the local church or the ignoble one of commitment to personalized consumerist Christianity—we have lost the grand scope of the entire family of God. While Christ calls people from all tongues, tribes, and nations, we have become content with our own tongue, tribe, and nation. Many churches are wonderfully embracing the imperative of a missionary mentality, but as they seek to own the mission by adapting their church into a missional movement in their local community, some inadvertently localize God's mission itself and lose the vital connection all believers share together. A hyperfocus on our own community results in a lost vision for the communion of the saints.

Turning Our View to the Culture

Transformational Churches fully embrace missional without losing the mission. How? First, they recognize it is God's mission, and they are passionate about the mission as He describes it. We don't own mission, and it is not ours to define. A church vision statement is fine, but God's mission is better and bigger. The first task is to submit to God's mission. They realized that church is not the center of God's plan. But, the church is central to God's plan.

Second, TCs understand and obey God's call to serve the poor and the hurting and are not afraid of a stronger engagement in social justice. This sounds counterintuitive if we are seeking to remedy the loss of concern for articulated evangelism. But social engagement entails relational engagement, and relational engagement entails opportunities to share the gospel. The successes and experiences in our communities should awaken hearts and minds to global needs. We just need to maintain the reason for social justice: the glory of God in the worship of Jesus.

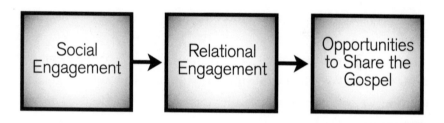

Third, TCs share God's deep concern about His mission to the nations—that His name be praised from the lips of men and women from every corner of the globe. They feel the Great Commission in their bones. Ask God to turn your heart to those you cannot see. As Paul did, develop ways to "struggle personally" for those far away: "For I want you to know how great a struggle I have for you, for those in Laodicea, and for all who have not seen me in person" (Col. 2:1).

Fourth, TCs are serious about joining God on his mission and obey his commands to disciple the nations. The end product of missional endeavors should be a thriving Christian ready to produce more thriving Christians. It appears that many missional churches fail to be Transformational Churches because they are missing the Great Commission in the name of being missional. That makes zero sense. It is a huge (but historically common) mistake.

If we are truly interested in being a Transformational Church, then our efforts should actually reflect God's mission. We are bound to the Great Commandment as the fullest human expression of God's love. But the Commandment is not hermetically sealed off from the Great Commission. Rather, the Great Commission provides the *what* of mission while the Great Commandment provides the *how*. Answering the age-old question, "Who is my neighbor?" should result in the desire to "make disciples of all nations."

> **If we are truly interested in being a Transformational Church, then our efforts should actually reflect God's mission.**

Transformational Churches are truly Acts 1:8 churches. They have a mindset to be a missionary in their community and ultimately to the entire world.

Of course these churches do not become missionaries without embracing key values. We will examine the first of these values in the next chapter. And we will learn how critically important vibrant leadership is to Transformational Churches.

4
Vibrant Leadership

"Whoever wants to be first among you must be your slave; just as the Son of Man did not come to be served, but to serve, and to give His life—a ransom for many."

(Matthew 20:27–28)

BY THE NUMBERS

"Our church leadership makes sacrifices
for the direction God has given our church."
(81 percent members strongly or
moderately agree)

Discovering Vibrant Leadership

Pastor Sean Park had a vision for vibrant leadership. In 2001 he planted Charisma Church in Raleigh, North Carolina, where it meets on the campus of North Carolina State University. Pastor Sean Park's passion for young disciples led to the birth of the "Charismax" internship process.[1] The process has resulted in the multiplication of many vibrant young leaders. Charisma is not for faint of heart. The one-year discipleship process is intense. Primarily geared to eighteen to twenty-five year olds, the mission is clear:

> To develop a life-changing ministry where young people can come to know Christ, establish strong relationships with their parents, fulfill their God-designed destinies, and change the world.

Ministry training, intense discipleship, and office work are part of the experience. Assisting with retreats and events is also included in the fifteen to twenty hours a week expected of Charismax interns. A part of growth is experiencing ministry leadership on every level. Spiritual disciplines, time management, basic doctrine, and the study of revivals are included in their OGSM (Objectives, Goals, Strategies, Measures for Life) study tract. Interns meet in small groups and one-on-one mentoring relationships. They are accountable for lifestyle expectations, morals, physical exercise, spiritual disciplines, keeping up with studies, and personal goals.

How does Pastor Park know Charismax has a transformational effect on young interns? He listens to how their stories change over time. Evidence of changed lives and perspectives abound. Many interns are now in full-time ministry around the world as missionaries, pastors, or worship leaders. God uses the Charismax to deploy vibrant leadership through Charisma Church worldwide.

TRANSFORMATIONAL LEADERS SPEAK . . .

"Many pastors and leaders do gain a true vision of their church from God but they struggle to turn vision into reality. These leaders may have experienced God moving in incredible ways throughout their church. But instead of helping facilitate that move of God with appropriate structure, it fizzles out with little more than a moment of momentum. . . . If structure is not added to what God starts, the powerful momentum can be short lived."[2]
—Tri Robinson, *Revolutionary Leadership: Building Momentum in Your Church through the Synergy Cycle*

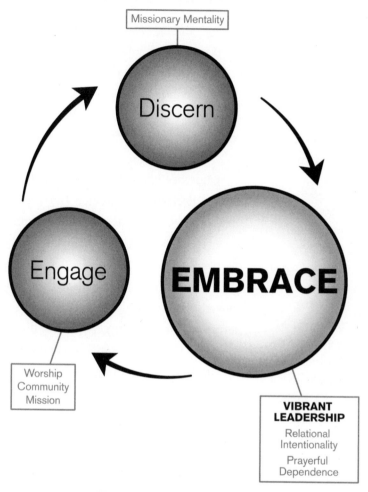

Missionary Mentality

Discern

Engage

EMBRACE

Worship
Community
Mission

**VIBRANT
LEADERSHIP**
Relational
Intentionality
Prayerful
Dependence

Transformational Loop

Introduction

As we worked through the research, we continually saw the importance of godly and vibrant leadership. Whether a strong senior leader, elder team, or staff team, vibrant leaders were always present in TCs. Vibrant leaders lead their people to worship, live in community, and live on mission. Transformational Churches are led by transformational leaders who are being transformed in the presence of the people they lead.

A Major Dilemma: Failure to Launch

Changing majors is common among U.S. college freshman. Recent research suggests that up to 80 percent of college freshmen will change majors before they graduate, some two or three times, causing 40 percent of college students to experience a "failure to launch"—going to four-year colleges between five and six years. This indecision creates esteem issues in students as well as a major strain on parents, their checkbooks, and the education system.[3]

> *Transformational Churches are led by transformational leaders who are being transformed in the presence of the people they lead.*

Churches, like college freshman, often struggle with declaring their major. The consequence of their indecision causes a major dilemma. The issue separates most churches from the TCs we discovered. Most churches suffer from a failure to launch (new or established) and stay the course. With no clear sense of purpose, they never set a clear strategy. What they do to fulfill what they think God wants constantly changes. They languish in seeming shadow-lands where forward momentum always seems one step out of reach.

Transformational Churches have leaders who understand their vision and purpose. A clear desire for changed lives is part of the new scorecard (discussed in chapter 2). They are not always looking for another "thing" to try for faster results. TC leaders instead watch and learn from the best practices of others to inform an already clear understanding of their context. What works for Rick Warren in California or Johnny Hunt in Georgia may not work for Pastor Bob in Ohio.

Transformational leaders let God shape their churches. As Christ is formed in individuals, the same Christ is formed in a church. The Transformational Church is Christ being presented to the community. TCs are tenacious about the vision and are people focused. TC leaders are focused on the mission of God for their church. Their leadership is multiplied with a different kind of agenda. What does the agenda look like? The agenda of a TC leader is based on a core belief that God has sent us on mission.

The disciples received the postresurrection commission from Jesus, "Jesus said to them again, 'Peace to you! As the Father has sent Me, I also send you'" (John 20:21). His purpose for them was not a warm, fuzzy "discover a brand-new you" or "run after your dreams." Jesus moved His disciples outward on the mission of transforming the world through His gospel. TC leaders are captured by this vision and lead the people in it.

Members in TCs, compared to members in other churches, were keenly aware of the vision of the church. In TCs, 69 percent strongly or moderately agreed that they knew the vision.

Understanding Transformational Leadership

Transformational leadership is more than the traditional, compartmentalized approach to ministry in the church. The mission of God is a priority rather than just one thing among many things. In the fall of the year, many churches place a special emphasis on missions as an international endeavor. But the reality is missions at best is only an item on a laundry list of important things at most churches. Missions as one thing among many things misses the heart of God. Missions treated like a sentimental switch that is flipped on during the summer and fall limits our transformational potential.

Transformational leadership understands that the church exists for the mission of God, and God gives leaders to help churches focus on the mission. Missions (with the "s") is focused more on the global tasks. The tasks are biblical: praying for missionaries, preaching about missions, going on mission trips, taking special offerings, and so forth. We need more missions, missionaries, and mission-focused churches. Yet, that is not enough. We need to be mission-minded

> *Transformational leadership understands that the church exists for the mission of God.*

and missional. And, that's a leadership issue. The change from only being a "missions supporting" church to a TC should not be complicated but must begin with an emphasis on the leadership encouraging people toward mission. That may mean emphasizing some things and leaving other things behind.

Maybe a new application to an old illustration will help clarify the difference between missions and missional. Remember the chicken and the pig's collaborative effort to provide breakfast? The chicken offers a donation, but the pig makes the ultimate sacrifice, right? The chicken (missions) has inspired some to give "some of me" while the pig (missional) is giving "all of me." In TCs the leaders are missional and will gladly die for the mission of God. They are all-out.

TC leadership focuses on leveraging every life for the kingdom of God around the world. Leadership emphasizes the need to be and do. Rather than a false dichotomy of formation or action, it embraces the need for both. TC leaders take the church on mission while creating a culture that owns and joins God in that mission.

Leadership might be the most confused term that we use in the body of Christ. We all assume a picture of leadership when we hear the word. Normally, what we really mean when we say "leader" is a strong, no-compromise, CEO who is not afraid of anybody but God. That leader is charging forward with a tribe of crazed followers. The leader has game show-host public charisma and a personality that makes even casual contact inspirational. The leader has a strong belief in personal leadership skills. He is always courageous and sometimes reckless. Before we go too far, understand that some of the above qualities are positive and important to the kingdom. But the subject here is not leadership. The subject is transformational leadership.

How is it different from other approaches to leadership? Transformational leadership is focused on the outside of the leader's world. Leaders may be charismatic and inspirational, but a centrifugal (outward) influence defines their leadership. A natural leader draws people in and sends people out. TC leadership is missional in perspective and action oriented in decisions.

A natural leader attracts and gathers other leaders. The TC leaders we discovered in our study multiply and scatter leaders around the world. Instead of promoting self, they promote the mission of the church. How many people who hear the sermon or attend the local church service are secondary. Note we said secondary, not insignificant. TCs, although their locations and size vary, are all about building disciples through a local congregation. Does a TC leader want more people to attend the local church? Absolutely! Leaders want more people because they want to send more people back into the community and the world. The focus of passion for a TC leader is for lost people not bigger churches.

Pastor Chris Ruppe of North Rock Hill Church in Rock Hill, South Carolina, led the church on a vision campaign. With the church located near Charlotte, North Carolina, his vision was for both Carolinas, just more than thirteen million people. Thus, Vision Carolina was born.

The goal is for North and South Carolina to be the first states to experience a faster conversion rate than population growth rate in the next ten years. The vision required North Rock Hill Church to enhance their sending and resourcing DNA. The vision began with them and their city. Each small group has a mission. Their partnership with local schools involved the vision to help every school in their county partner with a local church. The vision also included adoption and foster care for the children in their county. Their church planting coaching centers have multiplied to influence planters in their community as well as the world. They hope to reproduce the same DNA in church planters and remissioning pastors in order to impact other cities. The vision is missional and transformational. Over the next ten years every aspect of the vision, even the multiplication of campuses, is pressing outward from their current location. "We had a clear call to create a greater presence in our community. Developing campuses around the city will create an impact in those areas simply by our being there," said Pastor Ruppe.

Shift in Thinking

The key word is *transition*. Churches must transition from a segmented and tepid missions program to a missional church with vibrant leadership that leads the whole church to engage in the mission of God, locally and globally. It is not as simple as a new vision statement or a sermon series. The church is God's missionary seeking transformation of people and the community. When the church assumes the role of missionary, a radical shift in the view of leadership must take place. The old model was to hoard and retain control. Transformational leaders seek to empower and multiply. They think in terms of movements of God versus seasons of high attendance. Patience is critical. Courage to release and trust God is indispensable. To get moving in the right direction four mindset shifts are needed.

> *The church is God's missionary seeking transformation of people and the community.*

The first mindset shift toward transformational leadership is from one to many leaders. The CEO "Superman" model must be replaced by assigning a higher value on every man and woman. One reason churches implode is because of the overpromise suggested by our "Superman" view of pastoral leadership. Our professional Superman pastor will be trained in exclusive places called seminaries to gain expertise in business, family therapy, communication, marketing, leadership, and theology. The pastor will be taught how to lead local teams to spectacular church growth. A congregation has incredibly high expectations of their Superman. Superman returns the favor by having incredibly high expectations of the congregation.

But when the dream is not accomplished, finger pointing begins. Both the pastor and the members contribute to the finger pointing. Angry pastors bemoan the terrible people in their congregations. The pastor demands unilateral command and control. Then the church demands a high level of customer satisfaction, fiscal stability, and numerical success. And no one gets what they want.

TCs have strong leaders. Their leaders understand the importance of every man and every woman. Superman is for comic books, not for the body of Christ. We fear that church leadership has devolved to a counterproductive, bishop-driven system. The result is a disengaged, underchallenged, and underutilized missionary workforce.

When we surveyed TCs, we asked for them to agree or disagree with the following statement: "Our church has a system in place to raise up future leaders." That's a specific and challenging statement.

To our delight, 53 percent agreed strongly or moderately with the statement. To see that members, not just leaders, perceive such a system in their churches is an encouraging sign. Leaders in TCs are actively seeking to expand influence rather than hold it for themselves.

Transformational leadership pushes people outward. One example is First Baptist Church, Gallipolis, Ohio. It has enjoyed transformational results. More than seventy of the children raised in their church are now actively involved in ministry. Missionaries, pastors, Christian schoolteachers, Bible college teachers, and seminary professors are some of the ministers who began their early years at First Baptist Church. It illustrates the force of God's Holy Spirit sending people away. The Christian school affiliated with the church has also been significant in providing leaders in the community. Many leaders in the area are graduates of the church's thirty-year-old Christian school. Pastor Alvis Pollard said, "I can't go to the hospital without seeing doctors who are graduates." The church has provided leadership and leaders for the cause of Christ. The entire culture of the church is one of multiplication, sending, and scattering missionaries worldwide.

> *Leadership is the stewardship to help others exercise their gifts, not just an opportunity for me to exercise my gifts.*

The second mindset shift toward transformational leadership is from "me" to "we." Transformational leaders know that every person can be used to fulfill God's mission. Leadership is the stewardship to help others exercise their gifts, not just an opportunity for me to exercise my gifts. Clearly stated in Ephesians 4, the pastor's role is to equip. The pastor must have a vision to help others align with God's mission. As others succeed, God is glorified, and the mission of God is extended.

God spoke clearly through Peter when he wrote, "But you are a chosen race, a royal priesthood, a holy nation, a people for His possession, so that you may proclaim the praises of the One who called you out of darkness into His marvelous light" (1 Pet. 2:9). Simply put, "You" are the method for the mission of proclaiming God's praises. The transformational leader leverages the giftedness of people for the kingdom of God. "Based on the gift they have received, everyone should use it to serve others, as good managers of the varied grace of God" (1 Pet. 4:10).

The transformational leader thinks team. Everybody has a purpose. No one person's personal purpose is more important than the biblical purpose of the team. The pastor may be the coach of the team. Coaches recognize the need for people to get into the game. A football team cannot survive with a quarterback and a running back only. Linebackers, kickers, and linemen are needed. A football team cannot win with a hall of fame coaching staff but no players. TCs have found a way to "win" by engaging every believer into the work God has assigned to them.

My first venture in team building took place while I (Thom) was still a twenty-something young husband. Due to a variety of reasons, not all of them based on merit, I was promoted to vice president in a large bank holding company. The particular bank where I worked was in a small city about an hour from the bank's corporate headquarters. My responsibilities included the bank's commercial loan portfolio and the people who worked in that division.

After I left the corporate world to answer the call to vocational ministry, I had the opportunity to build teams in four different churches. The churches were significantly different in size, communities they served, and locations. As senior pastor I dealt with issues of integrating existing ministry staff with new staff that I presented to the church.

My next stop was in the world of academia, where I had the unique opportunity of starting a graduate school. That particular assignment was as Dean of the Billy Graham School of Missions, Evangelism, and Church Growth of Southern Seminary, so I was not without resources to begin this venture. Still, I had the exciting task of forming my own leadership team, bringing in a world-class faculty, and hiring administrative support personnel. One of the challenges was the time line. I had only six months to recruit the team, develop a degree program, seek accreditation, and recruit students.

Another team-building opportunity I had was starting a consulting company. I took the advice of several mentors in the secular world and kept the company's overhead low. In essence I was the only full-time employee, but I formed leadership teams by contract for each assignment. Over several years I began to use the same ten to twelve consultants. Though they never became full-time employees of my consulting company, they did become a *de facto* leadership team.

My present leadership role is president and CEO of LifeWay Christian Resources, an organization with approximately seven thousand full-time and part-time employees. The company includes four major ministry business divisions: a 160-store retail chain; a large book publisher; a large resource company for churches; and Christian retreat centers in North Carolina and New Mexico.

The first-level leadership team includes eight vice presidents and me. Each of the vice presidents leads one of the major ministry business divisions or one of the major support areas of LifeWay. One of my first initiatives when I came to LifeWay in late 2005 was the shaping of the leadership team.

While there is significant variety in the leadership assignments I have experienced, I have seen four common themes emerge from building leadership teams: a compelling purpose, the right leader, the right team, and a conducive culture. The four characteristics I have experienced are simple but not simplistic. To the contrary, team building is certainly not an easy process. It takes significant planning, buy-in, and old-fashioned work.

While there are no perfect analogies from nonchurch leadership scenarios to church leadership matters, some of the principles do hold true.

The Transformational Church, like the teams noted above, must have a compelling purpose. And that purpose must guide the people beyond the inward work of the church. TCs have transformational leaders who raise up transformational team members who have a missional mindset. The transformational leader has the God-given responsibility, therefore, to create the church culture that is missional and transformational. The "me" in leadership becomes the "we" of the church body.

The third mindset shift toward transformational leadership is from personal power to people empowerment.

- "Our leaders seem afraid to step aside and hand off ministry to others." (only 26 percent agree)

Our survey discovered that members and leaders in TCs are not only prepared to give away ministry, but they enjoy doing so. When we questioned people in TCs from a negative perspective, it confirmed what we were learning about these churches. In a TC fear of giving away ministry dissipates. Instead, TC leaders look for ways to hand off ministry to other people.

Pastors and leaders traditionally measure leadership by power. But power is overrated, particularly when it comes to deploying missionaries through a local church. Power must hold people close. When a leader has all the power, the people are demotivated to act. Powerful leaders make people skittish about making decisions. TCs decentralize decision making. Permission is given to act and to lead. This feeds a new scorecard. Service moves beyond the time block on Sunday mornings to the rest of the week. The church becomes an army of leaders advancing the gospel into the community. A transformational leader will celebrate community service as much or more than service in their local church.

The fourth mindset shift toward transformational leadership is from church to the kingdom of God. We are not deconstructionists who are tired of church meetings. God loves and values the local assembly of people called "church." Therefore, we do as well. But we find that leaders in TCs are as concerned with the wider work of God's kingdom as they are with

the localized work of their individual congregation. TC leaders know that the kingdom of God
births the church.

> *TC leaders know that the kingdom of God births the church.*

In the Gospels Jesus talked constantly about
the kingdom. The word *kingdom* appears at least
eighty times. The word *church* appears only in
Matthew 16 (its foundation) and 18 (church discipline). The church and
kingdom are related. The kingdom came first, and the local church is a tool
of it.

In recent days much has been written about the problems with
the church. We see people with chronic angst about the institutional
church. Certainly, the church organized has its faults. But problems in the
church began in cities like Corinth and Ephesus in the first generation of
its existence, not during the twenty-first century. Buildings and programs help the mission but can also become the unnecessary focus of a
congregation.

Whether by bricks and mortar, programs, or just the inward pull of
self, the church can become distracted from the mission of the kingdom. It
did not take long in the early church for the epicenter of God's activity to
move away from house to house and life to life. With the advent of church
buildings, the temptation was to become building-focused, inward, self-
absorbed congregations. People became spectators. Scattering throughout
the community as the church was replaced with the sacred, passive gathering in one place. The building and activities of the church at times became
more important than God's greater kingdom.

Competition, denominational worship, and sentimentality obstruct
the view of the greater kingdom even further. The real significance of
the assembly (people of God) is found in its place in the larger kingdom
of God no matter the building or generation. People are moved toward
God because of the vision for a higher purpose than mere assembly.
When church is reduced to that place on the corner where we go on
Sundays, we reduce the church and kingdom to something smaller than
God intended.

> *He was prepared to take the most unlikely of characters—the apostles—and make them the leaders of His church.*

TC leaders move God's people outward with the knowledge that God's expanding kingdom will help believers look more like Christ, the church will exhibit more qualities of the body of Christ, and their community will be impacted by the kingdom of God. The church on display is about people through whom God gets glory.

Paul lived out transformational leadership. He was an entrepreneur who modeled personal humility and tenacious will. But when Paul talked leadership in Ephesians 3, he couldn't stop using words like *gift* and *grace*. "His grace was given to me—the least of all the saints!—to proclaim to the Gentiles the incalculable riches of the Messiah, and to shed light for all about the administration of the mystery hidden for ages in God who created all things. This is so that God's multi-faceted wisdom may now be made known through the church to the rulers and authorities in the heavens" (Eph. 3:8–10). Again we see vibrant leadership as something inherently missional and intentional. A transformational leader has a resolve based on a real and ongoing encounter with God, not a desire to be "used" or known.

First, the Mission

In the aftermath of Jesus' crucifixion, the disciples were overwhelmed. One of them had betrayed the Lord. One publicly disavowed Him. The other ten had run into the night like frightened children. The formerly brave had become cowards. But Jesus appeared to them with a word of empowerment and a directive of mission. He was prepared to take the most unlikely of characters—the apostles—and make them the leaders of His church.

In the evening of that first day of the week, the disciples were gathered together with the doors locked because of their fear of the Jews. Then Jesus came, stood among them, and said to them, "Peace to you!" Having said this, He showed them His hands and His side. So the disciples rejoiced when they saw the Lord. Jesus said to them again, "Peace to you! As the Father has sent Me, I also send you." (John 20:19–21)

He gave them peace, purpose, and the Holy Spirit. It was a truly transformational experience. And Jesus is inviting the church of today on the same mission. And to the leaders, it is your responsibility to multiply your role based on the mission first.

The leadership shift we are witnessing is a new embrace of God's greatness displayed through us. TC leaders want those around them to say, "Now I know about this great God." Not, "Now there is a great leader." Transformational leaders have learned to trade in the small and trivial for substantive and eternal.

The Leadership Structure of Transformational Churches

We have established that the leaders of Transformational Churches are missional leaders. Missional leaders are focused on the transformation that comes from the gospel and the kingdom. They are personally engaged in the mission of God. A missional leader is constantly challenging people to move outward versus trying to gather them inward. The mindset shift on the missional leadership journey results in creating new leadership environments. Leaders are empowered and multiplied. Members are valued as God's greatest resources to fulfilling His mission. You will never hear, "Ministry would be great if it were not for the people," in these environments. Ministry is the people.

Believers work diligently at the mission of transformation because they are given real responsibility and opportunity.

In TCs, we found that people are excited about what is going on.

- "People in our church are energized by what we are doing." (68 percent strongly or moderately agree)

Believers work diligently at the mission of transformation because they are given real responsibility and opportunity. They are, as the survey statement suggests, energized by the work of the church. Why? Because witnessing the transformation of a person and a community is worth the effort to serve and lead.

What kind of structure supports such a leader and the mission of God? We looked at hundreds of churches that embodied specific transformational practices. We saw no consistent structure or template. We did discover the following substantive trends that were not context specific to size, model, or location:

1. *Traditional committees gave way to affinity-based teams.* A traditional committee approach was evident in some structures, but a more common approach was team. But even with traditional committee structures, those who served, served based on passion and giftedness. Some churches moved toward administrative or advisory teams that function in multiple roles. For example, in some cases nominating, finance, or personnel committees were combined into one team.

Pastor Jess Stafford of Eleventh Street Baptist in Shamrock, Texas, made the important transition in leadership structure. He led the church to team ministry as opposed to committees. Teams, according to Pastor Stafford, are formed as a result of people who have a calling from God. The calling is normally connected to the responsibilities of the team. To qualify for a team at Eleventh Street, you must have ability but also a calling from God to serve in a specific way. Populating the team with leaders is left up to the first people God calls to the team. The same criteria are used to finish the ministry team building process.

2. *Membership is encouraged to discover strengths, spiritual gifts, and talents.* Many churches had assessment processes where individuals can assess their giftedness. Coaching was offered by leaders to help members discover specific places to exercise their giftedness.

A Gallup poll conducted in 2002 produced some intriguing results. Church attendees were asked to report their level of agreement with the following statement: "In my congregation, I regularly have the opportunity to do what I do best." Over half the respondents did not strongly agree with the statement. One conclusion was, "Clearly, too many individuals talents and strengths were underutilized."[4]

PLACE Ministries is a resource originated by Jay McSwain, a real estate developer from Atlanta, Georgia. For more than twenty years PLACE has "helped people discover that God has created and gifted them with a unique capacity to serve others." More than nine thousand churches have benefited from the personal discoveries of everyday Christians. The PLACE process offers assessments to help discover how personality, abilities, spiritual gifts, passions, and experiences can be leveraged for greater mission.

Brentwood Baptist Church in Brentwood, Tennessee, requires every member to go through the PLACE assessment process and one-on-one coaching. One of their strongest Sunday School teachers (150 people attended the class) went through the process. Jay McSwain reported the surprising outcome:

> After PLACE he felt God wanted him to resign from teaching and go and put up a hot dog stand in the downtown area of Nashville where in a winsome way he could share Jesus with those in the tourist area of Nashville. When Mike Glenn, the senior pastor, heard about the teacher resigning, his first comment was "God will bring a new person to shepherd those people." Mike was elated that the man discovered what God truly intended for him to do in kingdom ministry.[5]

3. Churches had less structure as opposed to more structure. Many in our study cited the book *Simple Church* by Eric Geiger and me (Thom) as having had a major influence in revising their structures and processes. I am honored, but I am more encouraged by how it aids in the Transformational Church process. The result of less structure does more than enhance the church decision-making process. Less structure frees members from involvement in complex committees, councils, and ministries. Now people can be released to run after their ministry passions and callings.

Pastor Shane Bishop led Christ United Methodist Church in Fairview Heights, Illinois, to experience dramatic growth over a period of twelve years. The rapid growth caused the processes and structure to become complex. After reading *Simple Church*, Pastor Bishop determined to define their values more clearly and simplify their processes accordingly. Pastor Bishop said, "We think complexity would be our lid, we're going to have to simplify." Christ United Methodist and Pastor Bishop have taken significant steps in simplifying the expectations for their members. "Our mantra for membership is worship plus two. . . . That means we expect all members to worship at least once a week and be involved in at least one Bible study and then one ministry." Members pick one ministry and engage in service for one year. Then they go through a process to determine their ministry for the following year. They call the process Connecting Every Person in Ministry.

4. Structures reflect confidence in their pastor and positional leaders. Pastors of Transformational Churches were disproportionately either founding pastors of new churches or pastors who were long-tenured. Longevity and faithfulness produces trust. More trust is placed in pastors and teams for day-to-day operations. Congregations are less interested in micromanaging their churches.

> **Congregations are less interested in micromanaging their churches.**

Crosspointe Baptist Church in Concord, North Carolina, has a nine-person administrative team that makes administrative decisions. The group is empowered by the church to act on the approved budget and day-to-day operations of Crosspointe. Pastor Leon Hawks described the trust the congregation has in him and other positional leaders as "scary." Yet he also admits that "you don't violate that trust." He described the relationship between pastor and congregation as a "sacred trust." "As long as I don't violate Scripture, they're going to follow."

5. Congregation members did not vote on every issue. However, they were consulted on major issues. Not only was their perspective valued, but providing an opportunity for them to buy in was crucial to move forward.

Pastors described their churches as more congregational or worshipper led. However, church members did not micromanage, nor did they want to. Many churches in our study indicated a shift to less business conferences (once or twice a year). Congregations were consulted concerning "big" decisions only. The definition of *big* varied according to context. Property acquisition, yearly budgets, and major staff hirings were examples of decisions that were given to the entire congregation.

> *Members trusted their leaders for the day-to-day operations of the church.*

Westwood Alliance Chapel in Orlando, Florida, holds two congregational meetings a year. Pastor Jon Dunwell described how their leadership operated. Beyond the two meetings, "the rest is delegated power or authority, the responsibility by the congregation to the elders. . . . The elders have another team they work with called the ministry leadership team, which is made up of staff and other ministry volunteers."

Members must "own" the church in a positive way. Transformational Churches engage their members to help discover God's will and embrace God's vision. Some leaders mentioned their efforts to move back to a more congregational form of leadership due to the dysfunction of a strong, "top-down" style. Members trusted their leaders for the day-to-day operations of the church.

6. Small advisory teams and accountability groups worked alongside the pastor and staff. Some churches viewed these advisors as "elders" who helped oversee matters of the church. Other Transformational Churches considered their staff as elders and, thus, followed a staff-led model of church leadership. The trend toward greater accountability for pastoral staff is continuing. Although what inspired this movement was not clear, clergy morale and ethical failure clearly influenced the shift. Pastors have greater respect for their potential for failure. Most churches trust their pastoral leaders at times to a fault, but an accountability team sends a clear and positive message to their people.

Pastor Jamie Parker of Freedom Church in Carson City, Nevada, has an elder team that is primarily in charge of pastoral accountability. Pastor Parker said his board of elders "is the spiritual accountability that I need." He sees the need for a small group of people to keep him grounded. "If guys don't have accountability, you end with David Koresh and nonsense like that. . . . I don't want a cult."

Jesus, Leading Transformation

When studying the subject of transformational leadership, we should take a look at our own leader. King Jesus. He is the One who can best speak to the issue of leadership. We must be careful not to paint Jesus as simply a leader, or even the greatest of leaders. He stands uniquely as more than any human role. As the Son of God, we see in Christ every trait perfected and the only One who can purchase redemption by His sinless life sacrificed in our place. Therefore, we look to Him as our primary example of transformational leadership. Here are ten traits of Jesus, the transformational leader. As you read over their descriptions, take time to assess your own life and activity as a leader.

> *We look to Jesus as our primary example of transformational leadership.*

1. Jesus invested in people. Jesus invested in people because He believed in people. Paul described the trust God places in us as a sacred trust. He said, "We have been approved by God to be entrusted with the gospel" (1 Thess. 2:4). The word entrusted communicates the truth that God believed in the people to whom He gave the gospel. Jesus demonstrated incredible confidence in the potential of people to let Him use them for a higher purpose.

2. Jesus saw long and far. Jesus' leadership was evident in John 17:20 when He said, "I pray not only for these, but also for those who believe in Me through their message." Jesus was living beyond the moment. With the pressures of local church leadership, it is possible for us to shorten our sight. We must never reduce God's desire to inconsequential measurements. TC leaders are looking further than ever before. Instead of a two-year church calendar, we need to plan for the next century of impact. Jesus prayed for thousands of years into the future in detail for billions and billions of people.

3. Jesus sent people away from Him on mission. The transformational practice (to send away) continues to appear. Luke 9:1–2 and 10:1–2 give the picture of Jesus sending the believers away to do ministry. He sent them to touch the hurting and work for the harvest. The environment around Jesus was like an airport terminal. Disciples were constantly coming and going.

4. Jesus grieved for communities. "As He approached and saw the city, He wept over it, saying, 'If you knew this day what would bring peace—but now it is hidden from your eyes'" (Luke 19:41–42). Jesus was heartbroken over the rebellious nature of Jerusalem's inhabitants. Jesus wept over a community and calls us to love ours. "How often I wanted to gather your children together, as a hen gathers her chicks under her wings, yet you were not willing!" (Matt. 23:37).

5. Jesus led a balanced life. By the use of the word *balance,* we mean His perfect investment in multiple environments. Jesus knew the value of time away from the crowds. On several occasions He retreated from crowds to spend time with the Father. The Bible reports, "After dismissing the crowds, He got into the boat and went to the region of Magadan" (Matt. 15:39). He pulled away from the crowds to rest and pray.

6. Jesus embraced other cultures. Jesus embodied a cross-cultural gospel focus. He was not afraid of or offended by the Samaritans. He went out of His way to talk with them and refused to give up when they rejected Him. The heart of Jesus is for people, all people. It is illustrated by the life-changing conversation Jesus had with a woman at a well (John 4). The Holy Spirit birthed the church in a multicultural, multilingual environment. Acts 1:8 reminds us that we are commissioned to reach every culture and people group on earth.

7. Jesus gave up His will. Jesus surrendered His will to the Father. A transformational leader is in tune with the heart of God. He is not confused about who belongs to whom. Jesus prayed shortly before his death: "Abba, Father! All things are possible for You. Take this cup away from Me. Nevertheless, not what I will, but what You will" (Mark 14:36). His mission was to purchase redemption for us. We are not able to equal His work. But as transformational leaders, we must resolve to do whatever the Father requires. Jesus gave up His human will for God's higher purpose. So must we.

8. Jesus surrounded Himself with lost people. "All the tax collectors and sinners were approaching to listen to Him" (Luke 15:1). Jesus was attractive to lost people. He was kind to the adulterous woman (John 8:1–11) and Zacchaeus the tax collector (Luke 19:1–10). By offering grace and truth, the lost were drawn to be changed by Him. As much as we are sincerely driven to make our churches attractive, we must see the greater example in the missionary Jesus. The most beautiful element of our churches is people enjoying a transforming relationship with Jesus Christ.

9. Jesus' harvest vision was leveraged by prayer. Prayer is continually connected to the mission of God in the life of Jesus. We have no ability to transform anything without God's power. Jesus explained the power needed for the harvest was found in the resource of praying, "Then He said to His disciples, 'The harvest is abundant, but the workers are few. Therefore, pray to the Lord of the harvest to send out workers into His harvest'" (Matt. 9:37–38). The source for harvest workers is not in recruitment strategies, but in prayer. Prayer recognizes God as eternally resourceful.

10. Jesus felt the needs of people. Why did Jesus weep at the death of Lazarus (John 11:35)? Not for Mary, Martha, or the crowd to see. Simply because He grieved for the loss of His friend. Jesus was a man who deeply loved others. He felt their pain. Matthew 9 says that Jesus felt compassion because the people were "weary and worn out, like sheep without a shepherd" (Matt. 9:35–37). Jesus cared for people who were hungry and afraid. He cared for the physically sick and the spiritually oppressed. Jesus felt the needs of people.

Jesus came to serve the hurting (Luke 4:18) and save the lost (Luke 19:10). In Him we witness the greatest transformational leadership skills the world has ever known. But He did not provide a model because of His infatuation with the leadership image or culture. Jesus led out of His character and heart for the world. As leaders we are only display pieces of our Lord.

Transformational Leadership Environments

Transformational leadership calls for a shift from the single Superman to the importance of an empowered and released people focusing on the mission of God. The mind shift we have described allows a new environment to emerge. Let's look at its characteristics.

The transformational leadership environment values a team approach to ministry. Unnecessarily excluding people from the mission makes no sense to people with a big vision. Every believer is needed for the battle for every person. Each resource is precious because souls are precious. Leadership in TCs is not driven by independent entrepreneurs. Neither is the professional clergy the missions and ministry engine. Transformational leaders move beyond the clergy-laity divide and engage everyone for the mission of God.

> *Transformational leaders move beyond the clergy-laity divide and engage everyone for the mission of God.*

Satan has a simple mission: to keep lost people lost. Among his numerous strategies, one of his favorites is to keep Christians convinced that ministry must be left to professionals. But to reach the nearly seven billion people on the planet with the gospel, Christ intends to use all believers in the work. Satan attempts to convince believers that only exceptional people used in exceptional ways will accomplish God's mission. He would love for us to think that only the elite of leadership can be used in God's mission to save souls. But God's mission is for all Christians.

Leaders in TCs have discovered, uncovered, and recovered the biblical principle that God does not limit Himself to using extraordinary people. Extraordinary people for God are simply ordinary people who are willing to be used. Transformational leaders look for those ready to experience the exceptional rather than those convinced they are exceptional.

> *Leaders in TC have discovered, uncovered, and recovered the biblical principle that God does not limit Himself to using extraordinary people.*

The transformational leadership environment values a sharper mission focus. As a leader's mindset begins to shift toward a more missional approach, a new question emerges: Where am I leading God's people? God has some incredibly gifted leaders, and we need each one. TC leaders have discovered how to move people away from themselves and toward the mission of God. The difference between creating a follower and developing a leader is helping them understand and commit to the mission of God to make disciples of all nations.

When the mindset shifts, the focus will follow. The church will become more aware of the "big box" overpromise: Come to my church and be blessed by all the opportunities to grow. No matter how much your church provides it will never be enough. Spoiled baby Christians will always be disappointed. Pastoral leaders and their staffs will be emotionally broken down. God desires to energize His people to be on mission with Him. Unfortunately providing a carnival atmosphere through the local church seldom qualifies as His mission. I (Ed) recently drove by a billboard that featured an extremely large cut-out of a pastor's head. Next to the picture the caption read, "Over 135 ministries to meet the needs of your family." My mind connected the caption to a McDonald's sign that humbly reminds potential burger buyers, "Billions and Billions served!"

TC leaders are moving away from "How may I serve you?" to "How can I help you serve?"

In Luke 4:18–19, Jesus said, "The Spirit of the Lord is on Me, because He has anointed Me to preach good news to the poor. He has sent Me to proclaim freedom to the captives and recovery of sight to the blind, to set free the oppressed, to proclaim the year of the Lord's favor." Later in the same Gospel, we read, "'Today salvation has come to this house,' Jesus told him, 'because he too is a son of Abraham. For the Son of Man has come to seek and to save the lost'" (Luke 19:9–10). The incarnation was not to entertain those who were bored with life. Jesus' mission was to bring about redemption. Jesus' serve-and-save mission is given to the church. As a leader, it is your responsibility to guide people in fulfilling that mission.

The transformational leadership environment values new leadership priorities. Pastoral leaders are no longer me-centered leaders. The new priority is God-centered leadership. God by nature is a missionary God. He called us not to be great but to make His name great. How will that look? TC leaders will advance through the following steps:

> *TC leaders are moving away from "How may I serve you?" to "How can I help you serve?"*

1. *I join Him on mission or the "encounter" level.* Gone is the day of "do as I say." The new day is "do what I do." The transformational leader is an example and a model, not because he is supposed to be but because he is. When asked, 73 percent of TC members strongly or moderately agreed with the statement: "Our leaders remind me of Jesus." God has burned deeply within this leader his personal responsibility for the harvest. No more "do as I say, not as I do." Leaders personally engage the mission of God. The mentality here is, "I have had a real encounter with God. I want others to have the same encounter." They are the places where people could leave Sunday worship saying, "The pastor was a great communicator" but instead leaving saying, "What a great Christ."

2. *I lead others to join Him on mission or the "influence" level.* The priority in addition to personally engaging the harvest is also getting other people engaged in the harvest. The importance of influencing Christians to join the mission of God has growing significance to the vibrant leader. The transition here advances from a heroic, "Let me see how many people I can

get to heaven." The next step is, "Let me see how many people I can get to see how many people we can get on mission together."

Transformational Churches understand what is most important through the model of their leaders. We asked what created a difference in the way they practice church. The response was overwhelming. An astounding 76 percent strongly or moderately agreed with this statement: "While people may have different preferences, the vision God has given our church overshadows the different preferences." Having seen a difference in their leaders, the people were willing to give up on preferences in order to fulfill the mission. Only by a personal encounter with God and His work can this occur.

3. I lead others to lead others, to join Him on mission, or the "leading leaders" level. The previous level is the leading follower's level. This level is the leading leaders level. Leading leaders is a different skill set than leading followers. Followers are compliant and open to suggestions. Maybe they are followers because they are new in the faith. Maybe they follow because they are wired to follow. Followers are critical to the body of Christ and the mission of God. However, leading leaders is equally important. Leaders are led best by being engaged on the ground level. Normally leaders need much more information before they take action. Leaders are attracted to a compelling vision. The priority is to embrace different ways to approach leaders. Now the vision of the missionary leader is expanding away from him. The mentality is driven by the question, "What if I can get other leaders to be passionate about picking apples and about recruiting other apple pickers?" Now we begin to see influence over a greater area.

4. I lead others to lead others to lead others to join Him on mission, or the "movement" level. When God moves into regions resulting in large numbers of people converted to Christ and new churches started, then you have a movement. We consider this also the history-making level. The movement of God moves so far so fast, away from the original leader, that he cannot possibly get credit for the results. The major shift here is to a God-sized vision. However, the vision is calibrated to the size of lostness in the world. The dramatic shift is from, "What if I can pick an apple for God?" Now

the vision is, "What if I can influence leaders in multiple orchards to pick apples for God?" These multiple orchards will produce and harvest fruit for multiple generations of people groups everywhere.

The vision of God will never expand to this level without a deep level of engagement in leadership. The vision for one soul can be simple sentimentality and require little personal involvement. However, when God begins to reach cities and transform communities, a greater level of sacrifice is required. Our research revealed that TCs are populated with this type of leader. Note how many strongly agree:

- "Our church leadership makes sacrifices for the direction God has given our church." (81 percent of members of TCs strongly or moderately agree)

The reproductive environment needed for the mission of God is explained throughout Scripture. The desire to see this environment begins with a heart restless for greater results for Him. More and bigger programs will not provide a solution for the restlessness. The passion of TC leaders is for the power of Christ to transform entire communities, cities, and the world. They want to see the effects of the gospel multiplied throughout humanity.

Transformational Churches are moving outward with great force.

One explanation of the multiplication principle is seen in Isaiah 55. God is describing the preferred future for His followers. The vision God explains to exiles is one of hope, encouragement, and results! The people of God were exiled to a place they did not want to be, yet they had grown comfortable. God was calling them back home (Jerusalem), but it had become the rough and rocky place they did not want it to be. God explained His plan to provide perspective. Their exile was to help them understand and embrace His mission. "For just as rain and snow fall from heaven, and do not return there without saturating the earth, and making it germinate and sprout, and providing seed to sow and food to eat, so My word that comes from My mouth will not return to Me empty, but it will accomplish what I please, and will prosper in what I send it to do" (Isa. 55:10–11). Bread is a temporary solution. Seed is the bigger vision. The seed promised by God would result in perpetual bread for multiple people in multiple places for multiple generations. Their new, tough assignment to go home would be worth it!

Transformational Churches are moving outward with great force. Transformational Churches are populated by bold, missional leaders. Transformational leaders see the big things of God. God fuels movements through these leaders and churches. God is not calling leaders to be great. He is calling leaders to become platforms on which God displays His greatness. The mission of God is to display His power and glory for all to see. Thus, we have nothing to fear outside the room and away from the home base. The mission is all about Him, not us.

Because it is all about Him, these vibrant leaders are constantly leading people to develop relationships with the lost and hurting. This outwardly focused leadership is clearly following the example of Christ. And it's clearly transformational.

If vibrant leadership is one critical element of the "Embrace" facet of Transformational Churches, relational intentionality is another. To that issue we now turn.

5
Relational Intentionality

"For I want very much to see you, that I may impart to you some spiritual gift to strengthen you, that is, to be mutually encouraged by each other's faith, both yours and mine."
(Romans 1:11–12)

BY THE NUMBERS

There is a culture of inviting at our church, where people are constantly invited by others to get connected on a deeper level. (53 percent strongly or moderately agree)

Story of Success

Tammy is a fairly new Christian; she became a follower of Christ just four months before my (Thom's) research team interviewed her. She joined and was baptized in a nondenominational church near Scottsdale, Arizona. Our research assignment was simple: we were to interview new Christians who were active in churches. Our purpose was to get their perspective on the human factors that led them to Christ and to that particular church.

Our time with Tammy was a delight. Our initial and follow-up interviews lasted over ten hours. During that time we learned much about Tammy. And we learned much about the church that became such a big factor in her conversion story.

Tammy, a grandmother in her mid-forties, dealt for nearly a year with bitterness because her only grandchild had been taken from her home by a social service agency. She blamed the child's other grandmother for much of her troubles.

The crisis of losing the child and unbearable bitterness prompted Tammy to seek relief and answers. She started looking for a church though she rarely had attended church in her lifetime. She was fortunate because the first church she visited had a characteristic that is so closely tied to Transformational Churches: relational intentionality.

The leaders at the Scottsdale church had created an environment conducive to the development of relationships. Over the years many of the members of that church became highly intentional about developing relationships with men and women who visited the church and, especially, the unchurched who had never visited the church before.

Tammy was an unchurched person who happened to come to the church in a time of great need. The responsiveness of those in the church was remarkable. "I've never encountered this type of love and concern," Tammy told us. "I was blown away. I know that all churches aren't like this. If they were, the world would be a greater place already."

Unlike most churches that think they're friendly because they greet guests at church with a smile and a handshake, the Scottsdale church has become naturally relational. They don't have a program to be nice or to invite people to church. Instead, they are taking the love of Christ to hundreds throughout their community. They are turning the world upside down one relationship at a time. They know that people are not just looking for a "friendly church," they're hungry for friends.

TRANSFORMATIONAL LEADERS SPEAK . . .

"I believe the biggest reason Christians in general experience so little transformation in their lives is that they ignore the Bible's relational mandate for how to effect change. We were never meant to live the Christian life alone. Christianity is an interdependent, community-oriented faith. And yet when we set out to improve our prayer life, or deal with our anger problem, or increase our income, or become a better father; most of the time we work on it completely alone."[1] —Tony Stoltzfus, *Leadership Coaching*

Providing Relational Space for Uptown Charlotte

Watershed Church in Charlotte, North Carolina, is relationally intentional. Matt O'Neil and Scott Hofert started the church four years ago in a transitional area of uptown Charlotte. The contextual mix of the area includes the poor and young professionals. Public housing exists alongside expensive condominiums. Cabo Fish Taco Cafe operates near BJ's Soul Food Restaurant. In spite of the diversity of the people, they hold in common their lack of interest in church. The only chance Watershed has to break through is with intentional relationships.

> Space is provided for people to find and follow God.

To cultivate relationships in the community, Watershed sponsored a free movie in one of Charlotte's signature parks during each summer month. To pursue justice and mercy initiatives in marginalized neighborhoods, they organized home repairs, provided affordable Christmas toys for low-income families, and launched a program to provide support for families in one of the poorest elementary schools. Internationally, they provide tuition each year for twenty-five senior-high students in Malawi, Africa; they feed two hundred orphans a day and are financially supporting an ongoing initiative to dig freshwater wells. All of these initiatives provide platforms for new people to engage in significant relationships with one another and with people in need.

Everybody who attends Watershed on Sunday morning is considered a part of the Watershed community and mission from their first Sunday. Membership talk is avoided. Everybody, regardless of spiritual background, is invited to serve. Part of their relational intentionality includes a variety of connection points ranging from volunteerism (international service trips, internal and external ministry and service initiatives) and smaller communities called Blocs.

People who are spiritually inquisitive can connect and continue processing their spiritual journey. Space is provided for people to find and follow God. People are invited to deeper relationships the first day they walk in the door. They are personally invited into fun, informal relationships and immediately making a difference with their lives. To date, approximately 75 percent of those who attend Watershed connected in some sort of small group.

Discovering Relational Intentionality in Transformational Churches

Two concepts are married in this value: *relational and intentional.* Transformational Churches are highly intentional and focused. The same programs may be offered in other churches, but they are often an end to themselves. In TCs, programs are not the goal but part of a bigger picture of life change and mission. People are not projects or pawns to help pastors grow churches. They are loved and valued as people on a journey with Jesus.

> **People are not projects or pawns to help pastors grow churches.**

Bob Logan and Tara Miller captured the heart of a relational and intentional focus in their book, *From Followers to Leaders:*

> Both words—intentional and relationship—are necessary. As with many dialogues, we swing back and forth on the

pendulum. We either become so programmatic we lose sight of people and relationships. Or we become so purely relational that we don't accomplish anything. And the place to be is not just in between, but at both ends: both highly relational and highly intentional, with neither one watered down for the sake of the other.[2]

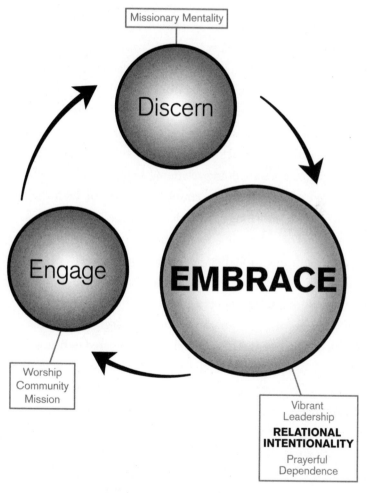

Transformational Loop

Churches seeking to help people look like Jesus, help congregations act like the body of Christ, and help communities mirror the kingdom of God accomplish this on purpose. TCs are intentional but relationally so.

The Practice of Relationships in Transformational Churches

No one system delivers relationships in Transformational Churches. Relationships can be intentional but are not a program. Could you imagine a staff position like *minister of relationships*? A relational approach to reaching and developing people is woven throughout every ministry and practice. Relationships are the substance of the church culture.

Pastor Chuck Williams, Live Oak Community Church Lubbock, Texas— The intentional, relational element is woven throughout each of their practices. Pastor Williams said that his focus on relationships is a greater emphasis now than ever before. According to Williams, "Relationships are everything. . . . We are doing relational evangelism, relational discipleship. . . . We challenge Sunday School teachers to be with their students outside the Sunday morning experience. . . . It is all relationships."

Even the act of welcoming a new person during the worship service in TCs is done with intentionality. We asked for agreement or disagreement to the following statement: "When people visit our church, there is a plan in place to ensure multiple people greet them."

The members of TCs strongly or moderately agreed with this statement at a confident 62 percent. These churches are prepared to bring new people into the relationships of the church from their first visit. Now, we realize that many churches have greeters at the doors on Sunday mornings. But TCs do so with greater intent than simply making sure everyone has a worship folder before entering the sanctuary. TCs greet people because they want to connect with guests relationally. In other churches the perspective is usually that it is the guest's responsibility to connect with the church.

Pastor Jon Dunwell, Westwood Alliance Chapel, Orlando, Florida— A relationally intentional element at Westwood Alliance is called Sunday

Munch. Once a month a catered meal is provided after the morning service. People already connected with Westwood make initial connections with new people. Members purchase meals for the new people who have yet to make the initial connection.

Pastor Thomas Sica, Open Door Baptist Church, Columbus Ohio— The intentional/relational element is a part of the environment from the moment people walk in the door. "Anyone can walk in our door and have a sense of comfort. . . . They could be a drug addict; they could have long hair; they could have tattoos all over their body. It does not matter to us because we want to reach you where you are."

Are Relational and Intentional Possible?

Defining *relational* and *intentional* as complementary terms is a challenge. The highly relational person is normally so by nature. Identifying what makes people (or a church) relational is difficult. Every church intends to be relational. TCs simply *are* relational. But because it is a natural attribute, being intentional about it is all the more complicated to identify. In fact, in most cases, highly relational people tend not to be overly intentional.

Now consider the highly intentional achiever. This person has skill with people but often sees individuals as part of the bigger picture. Intentional people (or churches) are visionaries who see the masses but not individuals. They are as passionate about tasks as the relational person is about relationships. Thus, the achiever sees people as a way to achieve.

The reality is both extremes have a dark side. The dark side of the achiever is to appear uncaring. The dark side of the relational is to appear irresponsible. As a communicator, the achiever is forceful and challenging. Normally such people are more prepared and calculated about what they are going to say. People admire the boldness and are inspired by the challenges. The achiever is leading a charge up the hill and running after a prize. The prize can be biblical and pleasing to God. The achiever is quick to measure results and make corrections for the lack thereof. Highly intentional people tend not to be overly relational.

The relational communicator is more warm and winsome. People enjoy the preaching moment when the relational communicator preaches. Personal stories are a big part of the Sunday sermon. The relational communicator wants to help you. The intentional communicator wants to lead you. The relational communicator helps you feel better about life, but you may not be challenged beyond "feeling better."

Churches will reflect the personalities of their leaders. Leaders create environments out of who they are. The church is no different. Its environment will be collectively shaped and influenced by the leaders. Some people are attracted to a highly relational environment. They are fueled by fun and fellowship. The relational environment becomes their best environment to offer Christ to their friends. Other people are attracted to a highly intentional environment. They are fueled by mission and projects. Both churches have a valuable place in God's kingdom but are limited from experiencing a real convergence of transformational practices because of what neither has.

> *The marriage between relational and intentional will produce transformed people who will populate Transformational Churches.*

What if we can marry these two concepts into one church? Remember, marriage is not the joining of two half people but the joining together of two whole people. Neither should be compromised, but both should be embraced, becoming complementary. The marriage between relational and intentional will produce transformed people who will populate Transformational Churches.

In these TCs, God is on display through filling the world with salt and light, highly influential Christians. Jesus described the process this way:

> You are the salt of the earth. But if the salt should lose its taste,
> how can it be made salty? It's no longer good for anything but to

be thrown out and trampled on by men. You are the light of the world. A city situated on a hill cannot be hidden. No one lights a lamp and puts it under a basket, but rather on a lampstand, and it gives light for all who are in the house. In the same way, let your light shine before men, so that they may see your good works and give glory to your Father in heaven. (Matt. 5:13–16)

We Are a Friendly Church

Over the years we have heard people all over North America describe their church as a "friendly church." But often churches only act friendly. Most churches measure the friendly quotient by internal preceptors of members. If their fellow members are friendly to them, they must be friendly to visitors. The way First Church of Friendly does relationships is radically different from a Transformational Church.

TCs move beyond sentimental friendliness. Greeters engage people arriving to worship. An enthusiasm permeates corporate gatherings. Participants' expectations are high. Energetic worship and an inspiring message from the Bible will be part of their experience. Excitement is in the air as people see, greet, and catch up with one another. TCs intentionally place a high value on relationships. Because of the value, they intentionally build platforms to create relationships.

> TCs intentionally place a high value on relationships.

The purpose of relationships is one of the dividing lines between the way First Church of Friendly (FCF) does relationships versus the Transformational Church. FCF does friendly in order to get you to come back again the next week. If your FCF journey includes a return visit, the scorecard changes. Hopefully you will join. Maybe you will give a percent of your income to the church. Hopefully you will serve on a committee or sing in the choir.

The purpose of relationships in the Transformational Church is to see lives changed through the power of Christ. Most people in churches can give the "good answer" to the "why" question of relationships. But TCs intentionally measure the results of relationships. They assess both quantitative and qualitative results. They provide processes to assess if relationships are producing life change. In a nontransformational church, *friendly* means "we are comfortable with each other and make good first impressions on visitors." Deeper relationships happen at First Church of Friendly, but they are normally born out of commonality alone.

People who join First Church of Friendly must be highly motivated. First, they have to fit in. Unfortunately the question FCF people think but dare not ask about them is, "Are you really one of us?" By nature we are tribal people. In other words, "If you look like us, listen to our music, think like us, and like what we like, you are welcome here." If newcomers pass the *fit-in* test, they become candidates for real acceptance into the membership as insiders.

The next step, once you are qualified, is to break in. FCF has a code to be really accepted. You must patiently, gently, break into the sacred areas of the church normally reserved for insiders. Part of the code is an *involvement code*. The qualification is: *Do you attend every church-based event offered in a given week that we (the core membership) value?* Never mind if you are new on the Christian scene. You may not even understand the incredibly high volume of hours some people spend doing church in a given week.

> The purpose of relationships in the Transformational Church is to see lives changed through the power of Christ.

Also you have to work through the *language code*. "Christianese" has been an oft-criticized habit of ineffective churches. TCs guard against the use of religious terms that could confuse any guest or even new believer. Theological terms are important to understand our faith but should be carefully explained to help people clearly understand.

Then you need the *building and grounds code*. Few churches have maps, clearly marked directional signs, and identified areas that explain where people need to go to engage something else. If you walk in the correct outside entrance door of many churches, the first time you attend you have to be either lucky or extremely smart. The bottom line: A friendly church and a relationally intentional church are two different churches.

Who Really Buys Friendly?

The Cypress Project is an initiative of North Rock Hill Church in Rock Hill, South Carolina, to create environments where God shapes leaders to reach cities and transform communities. Neal McGlohon is Networks Coordinator for the Cypress Project. He is a veteran church planter and coach. Over the past twenty years Neal has been on the ground floor of numerous high-yield, relational churches that reach a high percentage of non-Christians with the gospel.

Neal commented on the friendly environment as opposed to what seekers were really seeking:

> True spiritual seekers are looking for relationships. Church shoppers are looking for friendly. One reason church shoppers are satisfied with friendly is because their relationship space is already full. What does a true spiritual seeker want to know after the first visit to a church? They want to know if there is space for new relationships to help them along their journey. Most church people have no space to offer seekers, so seekers will simply "bounce off" the local church.[3]

How are relationships offered to seekers? Making low-hurdle invitations each week in the Sunday morning environment is one way. Also, regular church attendees need to be trained to find new people on Sunday morning and comfortably initiate conversations. Watershed Church creates environments where seekers are offered low-hurdle relationships. Early in the planting process they offered a Sunday lunch opportunity at a local restaurant. Discount coupons were offered as regular attendees invited new people to lunch. Each table at the restaurant had someone from Watershed to engage new people informally in conversations and to help connect them to next steps in the church.

Pastor Jon Dunwell of Westwood Alliance Church has created a more formal way to be relational and intentional. "Invest in the Next" is a meeting offered to people new to Westwood each Sunday morning. The meeting is led by two elders who are particularly good at making relational connections. They focus the meeting on assessing where people are in their relationship with God and what their "next" step is. Also, the meeting helps people consider their next step in making connections with the church. Follow-up assignments are offered each week (four-week class) such as investigating potential small groups. The whole idea is to keep new people moving through a process of finding and following Jesus. Although Westwood wants to be a comfortable place relationally, they do all they can to keep people from stalling out. They keep people moving on their spiritual journey.

> *If the only options for becoming an "insider" at your church are to fit in or break in, then your environment needs some serious attention.*

Do most leaders want their church to be a comfortable environment for people who are far from God? The debate is filled with contradictions. No matter where you stand on the seeker-friendly or seeker-sensitive spectrum, there are principles on which we all can agree. First, if the only options for becoming an "insider" at your church are to *fit in* or *break in*, then your environment needs some serious attention. Second, the cross of Jesus Christ and spiritual things will be uncomfortable to some people who are far from God no matter what we do. Paul reminded the Corinthians: "But the natural man does not welcome what comes from God's Spirit, because it is *foolishness* to him; he is not able to know it since it is evaluated spiritually" (1 Cor. 2:14, italics added).

We don't make this point to encourage a victim's mentality that many Christians seem to have. But we should know we cannot make every unbeliever feel comfortable about our message. The word for *foolishness* means "silly or stupid." No matter how seeker oriented we want to be, we must never disguise the cross of Christ. With great care we should intentionally explain the gospel and all its implications. But there is a corresponding relational element. The cross should be the *only* stumbling block any "outsider" would ever face when entering our churches. God's Word gives clear space for the cross to offend. The church is not. Creating comfortable, safe, relational environments is key to making space for new people.

Mayor Ed Koch of New York (1978–1989) was famous for a question he asked often in New York City Hall. He often greeted people with the brave question, "How am I doing?" Too many churches have a feedback phobia. TCs, on the other hand, look for outside assessments. They value asking the question, "How are we doing?" because they understand that much of the answer will come out of the relationships that have been built.

Most churches settle for a much safer question: "What are we doing?" It reduces the scorecard to activities or tasks. The assumption is that busy churches are successful. TCs and their leaders are obsessed with the details of God's work. But they push themselves to fulfill God's work in the midst of people. After all, without the impact on human beings, we are only playing church. Life change can be measured and should drive a church to assess consistently internally and externally.

> *Creating comfortable, safe, relational environments is key to making space for new people.*

Cincinnati Vineyard was tenacious about assessment. Founding Pastor Steve Sjogren was so concerned about the environment of his church that he chose to engage people he was trying to reach in genuine assessment. Cincinnati Vineyard paid people who were not Christians to experience Sunday morning worship and answer a few important questions in writing. Both relational and intentional were clearly at work during the assessment of the Cincinnati Vineyard Sunday morning environment. The assessment was relational because it valued the subjective opinions of individual and random people. The assessment was intentional because there was an agreement, at a point in time, with a desired outcome. Self-assessment takes courage, but churches that are relational and intentional will see the value far outweighs the discomfort.

The Look of a Relationally Intentional Environment

Unique variables exist in every situation that makes relationally intentional environments a challenge. A cookie-cutter approach would not have the same results everywhere. Unique obstacles exist. We will suggest a few of those obstacles, but first let's start with two important questions:

1. What are the challenges within your church environment to cultivate relationships, and how can you address them?
2. What are the challenges in your church environment to intentionality, and how can you address them?

Your unique local culture can be a challenge to cultivating relationships in your church. By nature people in your area may be more reserved or cautious. Another challenge is the current relationships your people may be managing. For example, if most of your church family is living in areas where they were born and raised, they have time-consuming family and extended family relationships. If a large number of church attendees have been involved in their current church for many years, those relationships take up space for new relationships. Work, weather, and recreation are issues to varying degrees in various communities. All these will challenge relationships.

One critical factor to transition your church to a transformational path is to teach your people about how to create relational space. In our survey we found that members of TCs gave significant agreement to the statement: "Newcomers to our church are tactfully yet purposely connected to a small group."

Leaders and members in TCs know it is crucial to move new attendees into significant relationships with members of the church. Therefore, we found that 71 percent of those surveyed agreed with the above statement. No matter how "simple" your church structure or process might be, your leaders will have to sacrifice in order to create space in their lives to do life in smaller groups. TCs have willingly made that sacrifice.

But a prerequisite to teaching *how* to create relational space is to teach *why*. We are not implying people can be guilted or manipulated into making more space. A high level of commitment and conviction will include substantive change. Offer time management help. Tell stories of your own relational efforts and those of others. Let them encourage one another as they transition by setting up peer-to-peer coaching. Remind them if God is leading them to make more space for relationships that some things will need to be eliminated to make space.

What do relationally intentional environments look like? What principles are transportable regardless of size, location, and denomination?

1. Relationally intentional environments produce family. Family language is common in the New Testament. The challenge is to build biblical family without creating a closed group. Yet building family or community is a critical ingredient of the relationally intentional church. In today's culture family images represent pain and disappointment in the lives of many people. The family of God can become a place of hope and healing. The local church can provide unconditional love and nurturing environments that people have yet to experience. Also, family produces an environment of accountability. Terms like "doing life together" or "life on life" are common descriptions of living in community with other Christians.

The goal of the church—an intense focus of TCs—is to make disciples. The disciple-making task necessitates that people care about one another while they do it. Additionally, TCs have rediscovered that lost people hunger for deeper relationships. When they witness deeper relationships in the local church, a clearer path is made to understanding the gospel.

A prerequisite to teaching how to create relational space is to teach why.

Tim Keller, founding pastor of Redeemer Presbyterian Church in Manhattan, has experienced church in a diverse and displaced culture. Beyond his own church, which he began in 1989, he is engaging cities with church planting efforts worldwide. Keller described the communal nature of salvation. He feels it is a critical element to spiritual maturity.

We live in a culture in which the interests and desires of the individual take precedence over those in the family, group, or community. As a result, a high percentage of people want to achieve spiritual growth without losing their independence to a church or any organized institution. . . . There is no way you will be able to grow spiritually apart from a deep involvement in a community of other believers. You can't live the Christian life without a band of Christian friends, without a family of believers in which you find a place.[4]

Jesus approached relationships with deep tenderness and fondness. He dealt honestly with the disciples he so deeply loved. We see examples of closeness and intimacy alongside rebuke and correction. The Scripture describes Jesus' view of the church as familial. "For it was fitting, in bringing many sons to glory, that He, for whom and through whom all things exist, should make the source of their salvation perfect through sufferings. For the One who sanctifies and those who are sanctified all have one Father. That is why He is not ashamed to call them brothers, saying: I will proclaim Your name to My brothers; I will sing hymns to You in the congregation" (Heb. 2:10–12).

Paul approached new churches and new Christians as family. Paul planted churches in multiple locations in the Roman Empire. He felt a particular family bond to those he loved so deeply. He used the word *brother* more than 120 times in describing Christians and used *sister* on five occasions in his letters. He regarded himself as the spiritual father of those he evangelized and mentored in the Christian faith. Paul was transparent about the joys and discomfort of a spiritual parent:

I'm not writing this to shame you, but to warn you as my dear children. For you can have 10,000 instructors in Christ, but you can't have many fathers. Now I have fathered you in Christ Jesus through the gospel. (1 Cor. 4:14–15)

Look! I am ready to come to you this third time. I will not burden you, for I am not seeking what is yours, but you. For children are not obligated to save up for their parents, but parents for their children. I will most gladly spend and be spent for you. If I love you more, am I to be loved less. (2 Cor. 12:14–15)

My children, again I am in the pains of childbirth for you until Christ is formed in you. (Gal. 4:19)

Transformational Churches are comfortable doing life together. They also make plenty of space for new people to experience the benefits and responsibilities of being family.

2. Relationally intentional environments practice one-on-one relationships. Larger and smaller gatherings will never provide all that is needed for real transformation. What the larger groups begin through teaching, worship, and encouragement is completed by God in individual conversations.

Jesus often preached to large crowds, but the most compelling conversations with individuals were informal and seemingly unplanned. Maybe it is because they feel more personal to us as we read them. Jesus challenged people like the rich young ruler. He blessed Peter because of his insight about who Jesus was. He invited people into a relationship with Him, like Matthew. He comforted people like Mary and Martha.

Jesus often preached to large crowds, but the most compelling conversations with individuals were informal and seemingly unplanned.

Jesus' words to people in need were not all the same. Why? Because they all were at different points of the spiritual journey and facing different circumstances. Also, because of the unique wiring and backgrounds of people, they respond differently to certain approaches. The reality is "one size fits all" does not work. One important place that "one size fits all" does not work is discipleship. If we insist on all our discipleship being in large groups only, then we are going to miss the majority of our audience. Relational and intentional includes small-group and informal relationships.

3. Relationally intentional environments provide space for difficult people. Sadly, churches often have no place for recovering alcoholics, single mothers, or handicapped children. A couple considering divorce, a homeless man, or a young man struggling with addiction to painkillers has no place to connect. We assume our own spiritual and emotional health. We feel much safer around people who are at least as healthy as we are. God has not given us the option of pushing away the hurting.

I (Ed) remember a funny T-shirt that reminds me of a critical issue in our church environments. I think all of us should be forced to wear one just for the embarrassment and lesson. Maybe it could be a new Christian dunce hat. The shirt said, "Jesus Loves You But I am His Favorite." The thought caused a chuckle the first time I saw it. But on a sad note, we really do have favorites, and normally they are people like us. Jesus has no favorites, He loves everyone with a lavish, everlasting love. Even those we consider high maintenance or emotionally unhealthy.

James taught the inconsistency of faith and favoritism. In context he gave an example of favoritism that involved giving a rich man a better seat at church than a poor man. James said, "My brothers, hold your faith in our glorious Lord Jesus Christ without showing favoritism" (James 2:1). The principle is clear. Our sin nature may tempt us to be proud and happy when certain people show up at our churches. The same sin nature can cause us to be awkward and uncomfortable when others show up.

James challenged Christians to engage people in the margins of life: "Pure and undefiled religion before our God and Father is this: to look after orphans and widows in their distress and to keep oneself unstained by the world" (James 1:27). There is no question every member must be willing to minister because when God really moves, broken and hurting people show up. Notice this is what happened in the Gospels. One way you could tell that Jesus was in the house was that the marginalized flocked to see him (Mark 2). The outcast and marginalized need the compassion of Christ. TCs have made the decision to welcome difficult people into their gatherings and into their lives.

TCs have discovered that welcoming in the broken is a blessing and not a curse. They have made the decision to care for those in trouble because they want the broken to become sons and daughters of God.

4. Relationally intentional environments do have systems and processes. Systems and processes make relationships intentional in a local church. Relationships are not program driven. Programs can be relationship driven, however, and should be. Relationships are people driven. We don't want to replace natural relationships with programs, but we can champion relationships through them.

Yet program abuse by local churches is common. To avoid it, TCs make sure their programs fuel their God-given purposes, and they don't allow programs to replace relationships. When programs replace relationships, they become safe, dead, religious activity. The old evangelists used to preach, "Going to church doesn't make you a Christian any more than going to the garage makes you a car." Point well taken. One more point: "Going to a program doesn't make you a disciple any more than going to an Apple Store makes you a Mac computer." Attendance on every Sunday morning, Sunday evening, and midweek Bible study will not make a person into a mature disciple. Church relationships are necessary for that to happen.

> *TCs have discovered that welcoming in the broken is a blessing and not a curse.*

Intentional relationships fill in the cracks that we normally see people fall through in local churches. Systems and processes must provide a steady stream of intentional relationships to give life and fruit to your efforts. The systems and processes are built on ongoing biblical purposes.

General Motors has a vehicle assembly plant in Bowling Green, Kentucky. Visitors are invited to tour the facility. Once inside, guests walk along a painted floor path, watching the vehicle being assembled almost piece by piece. It begins with the chassis and concludes with the installation of the steering wheel. After a short stationary test drive, the back door opens and out rolls a beautiful new Corvette.

As the visitor stands at the door, no SUVs drive out. No trucks. No vans. Only Corvettes. This assembly plant knows exactly what they want to produce and have the systems and processes to produce such.

As church leaders, do you know what you want to produce, and are systems and processes in place? Most church leaders will claim the development of disciples is the aim.

- If our church were a factory, what would we be making?
- What would be along the assembly line to help produce the type of person God wants?
- How can we tell when you are doing a good job?
- What will a complete (not perfect) disciple look like?

What is the difference between a system and a process? Do you need both or just one? A system is an environment. A process is a path with a purpose. A system is a way of doing things. It provides the "how." A process is a destination. It provides the "where." For the greatest results, systems and processes must align. The most obvious example is making disciples. The vision to make disciples should have a clear supporting process unless you want to make disciples accidentally. The process has a destination in mind: a thriving Christian, a person who is connected relationally, growing in the knowledge of God's Word, serving in the church, and going out on God's mission regularly.

- "Our church constantly challenges people to take the next step in the discipleship process." (61 percent of TC members strongly or moderately agree)
- "If someone desires to serve in a ministry at our church, there is a clear and easy step to take to begin serving." (56 percent of TC members strongly or moderately agree)

Small groups might be a system along the assembly line. Within the system there is a way of doing things—rules, small-group principles and practices, plans to increase capacity, and so forth. But TCs know the purpose of small groups is to help people along the discipleship path or process. And they act accordingly. Small groups might be the main system in the discipleship process, but seldom is it the only one. Because small groups are part of the discipleship process, their basic DNA is the same.

One example from Scripture may give light to the role of systems and processes in the local church. We do not suggest this passage is biblical proof to defend systems thinking. The systems (and processes) put in place in Acts were not a result of the early church leaders going to a business seminar. But they are clear examples of how God builds a Transformational Church.

> *The process has a destination in mind: a thriving Christian.*

The purpose of church leadership was to evangelize through preaching and prayer in the book of Acts. Discipleship was also supported by the preaching and prayer ministry of the local leaders. Smaller groups delivered teaching, fellowship, and prayer. The result of this process: large group, small group, teaching, and disciplines; and all produced by multiplying disciples. Things were going according to God's plan.

But in Acts 6 we see the process of disciple making face a major production obstacle. Discontent members (Hellenistic widows) felt they were getting a raw deal. Note that the apostles did not take a "who cares, we are doing something more important" attitude. They addressed the need by creating a distribution system to ensure proper care for all of the widows. They put something in place that was relational and intentional in hopes that this would never happen again.

> Then the Twelve summoned the whole company of the disciples and said, "It would not be right for us to give up preaching about God to wait on tables. Therefore, brothers, select from among you seven men of good reputation, full of the Spirit and wisdom, whom we can appoint to this duty. But we will devote ourselves to prayer and to the preaching ministry." (Acts 6:2–4)

The system worked! The widows were too important to neglect. The work of the prayer and preaching was also too important to neglect.

Intentionality—led by the Holy Spirit—produced stronger relationships and thriving disciples. New servant leaders were empowered and released to take care of the widows. The disciple-making process produced more results: "So the preaching about God flourished, the number of the disciples in Jerusalem multiplied greatly, and a large group of priests became obedient to the faith" (Acts 6:7).

Conclusion

We believe, in spite of the obstacles faced by the local church in North America, that there is reason for hope. Yes, we are familiar with the numbers. We have written about some of the numbers as a result of our research. Yet in the midst of the great flood of lostness in North America, the dove has returned with an olive branch.

We refuse to follow the often-cited script of a doomsday church picture. If we will stay rightly related to Christ and to one another, the church in North America does not have to face decline. But we also feel a tremendous responsibility and stewardship. The local church is God's platform for His glory and His chosen delivery system for the gospel.

Every church has a system (way of doing things). Systems exist whether they are intentionally put in place or not. Each system has written rules but even more powerful, unwritten rules that every insider knows by heart. If relationships are God's chosen delivery system for evangelism and discipleship, then they are worthy of our highest focus and intentionality.

> *In the midst of the great flood of lostness in North America, the dove has returned with an olive branch.*

Relationships are the proverbial "hill to die on." But intentional and relational are often difficult to wrap our arms around. Intentional and relational look different in every context and face different obstacles. So . . . are you ready for this . . . in your context what will relational intentionality look like?

Pastor John Stallings created an intentional environment for relationships at Massillon Church of the Nazarene, Massillon, Ohio. He challenged his people to abandon judgmental attitudes that corrupt the relational environment. "We love people when they come in. . . . It's written on our business cards and a variety of other places. . . . We're a place for love, hope, forgiveness, and then mission."

> *The church is God's platform for His glory and His chosen delivery system for the gospel.*

"Love, hope, forgiveness, and mission" is more than a slogan; it outlines the intentionally relational process at Massillon Church. The critical first step is love. Stallings said, "Our job's to love people; God's job is to change them. If we step over into the changing part, then we're getting over on God's side." Many experience unconditional love for the first time. The result is restoration of hope and openness to the forgiveness of Christ. The entire process engages broken people who have experienced the forgiveness of Christ in the mission of God.

Pastor Stallings described the type of people who are a part of his church. "Our church has a lot of what most people don't want in church. If you've ever been a drug addict, if you've been a stripper, if you've been in jail, and even if you've . . . We're trying to reach a wide variety of people. I could look at anybody and feel comfortable in saying to them, 'Hey, come to our church. People will love you there.'"

Any church with a desire to be a part of God's great transformational mission should be described in the same way. "People will love you there." Any place where God has changed people is a place where people will love you.

Intentional relationships are at the heart of the gospel. Notice the welcoming environment surrounding Jesus: "All the tax collectors and sinners were approaching to listen to Him. And the Pharisees and scribes were complaining, 'This man welcomes sinners and eats with them!'" (Luke 15:1–2). Our mission is not an activity but a relational engagement with God.

Transformational Churches have determined that relationships are essential to the mission of the church. The mission is not a thing but a relationship with another person who is yet to meet Him.

Transformational Churches have determined that relationships are essential to the mission of the church.

Paul described the essence of the relational intentionality when he described Corinthian Christians: "You yourselves are our letter, written on our hearts, recognized and read by everyone, since it is plain that you are Christ's letter, produced by us, not written with ink but with the Spirit of the living God; not on stone tablets but on tablets that are hearts of flesh" (2 Cor. 3:2–3).

God's delivery system for the gospel is relationships with people who have met Him. Transformational Churches get relationships and do them intentionally because relationships are the platform through which people find and follow Jesus.

Embracing Three Values

Transformational Churches first "Discern." They see their communities and the world with a missionary mentality. The TCs also "Embrace" three key values. We have looked at two of those values: vibrant leadership and relational intentionality.

In the next chapter we discuss the third key value: prayerful dependence. Though we listed it third in three values, it may very well be the most important. With prayerful dependence, we recognize the true source of transformation. Read carefully this next chapter. It may be the key to beginning transformation in your church.

6
Prayerful Dependence

*I love the L*ORD *because He has heard my appeal*
for mercy. Because He has turned His ear to me,
I will call out to Him as long as I live.

(Psalm 116:1–2)

BY THE NUMBERS

Seeing people praying together is a normal
sight at our church. (73 percent strongly
or moderately agree)

Story of Success

"A lady, who was sick and wanted prayer, came to the altar. Her five-year-old daughter was with her. They were waiting for the pastor to pray for them. But before the pastor could get there the little girl put her hand on her mother and said, 'Lord, heal my mommy.' You want prayer to be something that's a powerful expression of faith and belief that God can touch those around you. Then prayer becomes a pleasure and something the body wants to do." —Robert Smith, Centenary Assembly of God, Luverne, Alabama

TRANSFORMATIONAL LEADERS SPEAK . . .

"I have discovered an astonishing truth. God is attracted to weakness. He can't resist those who humbly and honestly admit how desperately they need him."[1] —Jim Cymbala, *Fresh Wind, Fresh Fire*

God's Invitation to Tabernacle Baptist

In 1986 Tabernacle Baptist Church, Lake City, Florida, was in the process of closing its doors for good. Earnest money ($5,000) had already been given by a local businessman to purchase the facility. His plans for the building: to become a diesel mechanic shop. Mike Norman became the new pastor of a church with a deteriorating facility and a heartbeat away from death. The first five years were a struggle to the point that Mike and his wife had given up.

A Sunday night discussion of real revival led to a person volunteering his home for a prayer meeting the next night. A second person volunteered to host a Tuesday night prayer meeting. God moved in the lives of people in incredible ways. The first Monday night a young girl received Christ. Every night people would begin their story with the words "You are not going to believe what God did." Numerous stories of salvation, financial provision, and physical healing emerged from the meetings. Nightly prayer meetings started at seven and ran as late as ten each night.

The revival moved to Sunday mornings. Pastor Mike Norman kept a journal over eighteen months. During this period attendance and offerings tripled. Services ran as late as one in the afternoon. "We would start congregational singing, and folks would get up and just come to the altar," said Pastor Norman. "We had people saved during the singing. I just led the traffic; that's what I did." *Prayer is the engine of Transformational Churches.*

Discovering Prayer in the Transformational Church

A prayerful dependence is evident in Transformational Churches. These churches are humbly dependent on God for the vitality of the church. Prayer is not a program, and in many cases a weekly prayer meeting is not offered. Yet prayer undergirds everything a Transformational Church does. Researchers referred to prayer as the engine to the churches we identified as transformational. It sustains their worship. It is evident in their community (their relationships). Prayer fuels their missional engagement.

> *Prayer is the engine of Transformational Churches.*

Prayer has always held a significant role in the church. This is especially true of times the church is in the midst of revitalization or revival. Iain Murray wrote,

> What happens in revivals is not to be seen as something miraculously different from the regular experience of the church. The difference lies in degree not kind. In an outpouring of the Spirit, spiritual influence is more wide spread, convictions are deeper and feelings more intense. But all this is only a highlighting of normal Christianity.[2]

Prayer is not something that suddenly appears in a church because it begins to show transformational practices. The vast majority of churches we surveyed valued prayer. But the level, type, and expectancy about prayer in TCs was simply different. Similar to Murray's observance about experiences in the church, prayer in TCs is greater in amount and intensity.

God's intent is that believers—both individually and collectively—remain in close communication with Him. It is the reason He gave us prayer. We would define prayer simply as the volitional response of a person to listen and speak to God about His work and character. In order to see transformation occur in a person, church, or community, God must be involved. God must be invited into the story. Prayer is our link to receive understanding from God about His Word and move forward in obedience to His mission.

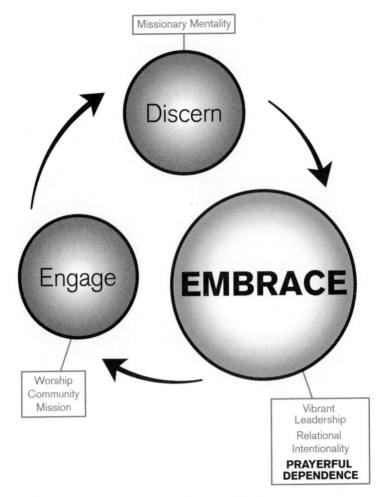

Transformational Loop

Transformation Findings

Conducting a survey on prayer is difficult. First we are faced with measuring the "effectiveness" or "success" of prayer as an activity. Quite frankly, we are reluctant to attempt such a measure. Prayer is a response to God's work rather than a fulcrum to move Him to action. Therefore, as we asked questions, we were faced with more qualitative answers (experiential) rather quantifiable measures (numerical).

TCs responded that prayer is a commonplace activity of the church. Other churches showed a penchant for organized prayer gatherings that are sparsely attended. For example, we asked for agreement or disagreement on this statement:

- "Moments of spontaneous prayer in worship services, groups, or classes are normal within the life of our church." (58 percent strongly or moderately agree)

Through the stories and the surveys, we found that prayer in a TC happens naturally out of the community of believers. It is done with expectancy rather than out of repetitive behavior.

Immanuel Christian Reformed Church in Fort Collins, Colorado, experiences worship services with different types of prayer woven throughout. Pastor John Terpstra includes a prayer of adoration in each service "invoking the holiness, greatness, and awesomeness of God." A prayer of confession is included that can be in unison or led by some-

> *Prayer is a response to God's work rather than a fulcrum to move Him to action.*

one. Specific times of intercession and even hearing requests are included. Also, prayer teams are available for people after the service where people can follow up with prayer concerns.

The work of prayer is central in a TC worship service. Once again we witnessed the convergence of the Transformational Loop elements when surveying prayer in the churches. In these places members know that prayer is the regular practice rather than an interruption to the norm. Through prayer they believe God will change lives.

Another discovery about prayer in TCs is its link to service.

- "Those who serve in our church spend time in prayer before serving together." (79 percent strongly or moderately agree)

TCs are intensely concerned with witnessing life change. To that end they refuse to rely on human ingenuity. With that being said, many of the TCs from our study are leaders in innovative and contextualized ministry.

But they know that only with God's work among them will individual and societal transformation take place.

A common story line would go like this: Mary coordinates greeters for this Sunday for her church. In the days leading up to Sunday, she calls all of those volunteering to welcome guests and members and asks them to arrive a few minutes early. When they do, they know they are coming to pray. Why do they know this? Because they always pray before people begin arriving to worship and Bible study. Why do they do this? In anticipation that God's presence, His work, and redemptive power will be palpable to everyone who walks through the doors. They pray for one another to be filled with God's Spirit and for the ministries of the church to reach beyond the campus on Sundays.

> *Through the stories and the surveys, we found that prayer in a TC happens naturally out of the community of believers.*

And they gather to pray without a mandate from the pastors, elders, or church council. They pray together before serving because it is the natural order of things in their church.

We spend profuse amounts of time speaking to churches across the country and have discovered a sad reality. Too many churches trust in their stuff and not their Savior. On the other hand, TCs pray before they serve because they want God to work through them and never in spite of them. They trust their Savior rather than their stuff.

One of the other measures for prayer is how often it is observed occurring by other parties. We looked for the perception of its frequency in churches.

- "Seeing people praying together is a normal sight at our church." (73 percent strongly or moderately agree)

Perhaps this is the discovery from the Transformational Church survey that best shows the difference between TCs and other churches. It is a good place to ask a tough question: "How common is spontaneous prayer in your church?" In a TC, prayer happens out of a history of what has been seen as its result. People pray in TCs because they have seen prayer bring about transformation.

What Makes Jesus Angry?

For some people the picture of an angry Jesus is uncomfortable. Jesus, holding a lamb, praying in a garden, or having a child on His lap is much easier to envision. In light of the holiness of God and the compassion of Christ, we can be assured heaven cares about the details on earth. God is not passive or soft. When people suffer or sin, heaven is grieved. God is engaging the world through His Son Jesus even as you read this paragraph.

Jesus displayed emotion in His earthly life. Jesus wept over Jerusalem (Luke 19:41) and at the tomb of Lazarus (John 11:35). Jesus felt compassion for harassed and helpless people (Matt. 9:36). And on at least two occasions Jesus showed anger. So what can we learn from Scripture about the anger of Jesus?

If you did not know much about Jesus, you might assume what would make Him angry. People who cheat people out of their money would be a safe assumption. He has to be really angry at Barney Madoff, right? Madoff is the former NASDAQ chairman currently serving a 150-year prison sentence for defrauding people of billions of dollars. Yet the Bible recorded Jesus' relationships with tax collectors, who in those times were known cheats.

Surely the prostitutes and others who were sexually immoral made Jesus' blood boil. From the brothels in Las Vegas to the multibillion-dollar porn industry, Jesus has to be pretty annoyed by it all. Yet we have no record of anything but love, hope, and forgiveness when He came in contact with a woman caught in adultery or another woman with a history of immoral relationships He met at a well.

Too many churches trust in their stuff and not their Savior.

A closer look at the two anger episodes in the Bible sheds light on things that make Jesus angry.

First, Jesus' anger is directed toward religious people. Conventional wisdom would assume religious people would be among Jesus' favorites. They are the lifeblood of spiritual movement. Think about it. Religious people think and talk about God a lot. They also have a lot of public meetings in honor of God. Donations to God's work flow from religious people. Oftentimes religious people are quick to defend what they think is in God's best interests. The entire religious operation should be in good shape as long as there are plenty of religious people to keep the machinery operating. Not so fast. Often in Scripture Jesus was direct and outspoken about the misbehavior of religious people. In essence, the misbehavior of the religious was terrible for business. At least twice their misbehavior triggered Jesus' anger.

In Mark's Gospel, Jesus met a man in the temple who had a withered hand. He was disturbed by what He knew the religious people were thinking. The religious people for technical reasons thought Jesus should ignore the man with the withered hand. The story told how Jesus responded, "After looking around at them with anger and sorrow at the hardness of their hearts, He told the man, 'Stretch out your hand.' So he stretched it out, and his hand was restored" (Mark 3:5). Jesus was angry at the hard hearts of the religious and sorrowful for their lack of compassion.

The second anger episode is told in all four Gospels. All of these accounts confirmed public expressions of anger from Jesus. Matthew's account in 21:12–13 is one example: "Jesus went into the temple complex and drove out all those buying and selling in the temple. He overturned the money changers' tables and the chairs of those selling doves. And He said to them, 'It is written, My house will be called a house of prayer. But you are making it a den of thieves!'" John's Gospel adds the word "zeal" to describe Jesus' response: "After making a whip out of cords, He drove everyone out of the temple complex with their sheep and oxen. He also poured out the money changers' coins and overturned the tables. He told those who were selling doves 'Get these things out of here! Stop turning My Father's house into a marketplace!' And His disciples remembered that it is written: Zeal for Your house will consume Me" (John 2:15–17). The word *zeal* means "fierceness of indignation" or "fervor of spirit."

So did Jesus lose control? Absolutely not. The Bible teaches that anger and sin are not necessarily the same. Anger can cross a line as it does most of the time with us. Then anger becomes sin. Paul was clear in his letter to the Ephesians: "Be angry and do not sin. Don't let the sun go down on your anger, and don't give the Devil an opportunity" (Eph. 4:26–27). Jesus is angry when we use His assembly for anything other than His intended purpose. Specifically He is angry when prayer is replaced by earthly activities. Jesus expects His people to practice praying and encourage others to do the same.

> *Jesus expects His people to practice praying and encourage others to do the same.*

If your vision for people is personal transformation, this will be seen in the practice of praying. Strategies, excellence, methods, or even commitment cannot substitute for humble dependence on God. If our motivation is numerical growth, then we have no real reason to pray. Organizational expansion principles will produce results relative to your community or "market." Teamwork, communication, people skills, and quality control will produce results. But none of these things will produce substantive results from God in the lives of people. Organization growth in the name of God will not save a marriage. Organizational growth will not free people from life-destroying habits. Organizational growth is a low bar. Transformation is His work. We cannot rely on ourselves and see transformation. It is impossible for us to affect life change in others. The temple was filled with people and activity. Yet Jesus was angry over what He saw. He did not see people engaging the Father in relationship.

Wayne Cordeiro is the founding pastor of New Hope Christian Fellowship in Honolulu, Hawaii. He has helped plant eighty-three churches through the ministry of New Hope in the Pacific Rim. In addressing our issue of self-dependence, he says:

> We don't know what God knows. The sooner we accept this, the
> better off we'll be . . . We rashly take matters into our own hands.
> We maneuver and manipulate to get what we want. We know
> it's not really the best, yet we'll show people the results and say,
> "Look what God gave me!"[3]

Prayer Priorities of Christ

As we embrace life with Jesus, we embrace His priorities. As we embrace His priorities, they will become our practices. Jesus demonstrated His passion for the proper priorities in His local assembly. Three priorities of Jesus are clearly violated in the scene at the temple.

1. *The proper use of His house.* When Christians assemble, they should pray. No matter the model or age of the church, prayer is a nonnegotiable. The earliest church included prayer in their daily routine (Acts 2:42). People should be called to pray in groups and as individuals when they gather. Invitations and opportunities to pray should be made in smaller groups as well as in the large assembly. Nothing is more important than God's people praying. Jesus said so.

> *As we embrace life with Jesus, we embrace His priorities.*

TCs see prayer as a critical part of changing their community. We learned in our study that prayer walking in the community was common. Churches offered prayer for people outside their church through various means. Prayer for educators, politicians, policemen, firemen, and other community leaders was practiced. Prayer groups, prayer vigils, prayer rooms, and prayer events happened consistently in Transformational Churches.

Notice the transformational influence prayer had on God's restoration of people and places. God was responding to the prayer of Solomon in 2 Chronicles. Solomon was praying a long dedication prayer for a newly completed temple for God. The building was amazing to behold (2 Chron. 3–4) and built to display the glory of God. For almost two chapters Solomon prayed for the presence and blessing of God on the building set aside for His purposes. The prayer included the request that God's eyes and ears be open to the prayers of His servants. God's answer to Solomon's prayer was immediate in the form of a challenge and a promise. God said, "And My people who are called by My name humble themselves, pray and seek My face, and turn from their evil ways, then I will hear from heaven, forgive their sin, and heal their land" (2 Chron. 7:14).

Notice healing did not stop with the individual who needed a fresh touch from God. When God touches His people, the ramifications are far-reaching. God promised He would heal their land. In the historical context of 2 Chronicles the "land" was not producing crops. God's people experienced His discipline because of their selfish, anti-God behavior. Yet, in principle, the same issue is being lived out in cities and communities throughout North America. Personal sin can have a public effect.

The solution begins from inside the church with the changing of God's people. When they change, He begins to use them to change the community, the "land." Seeking God's face and praying are significant steps in seeing transformation in your city. Pray for God to do transformational work on His people first.

2. The accessibility of "all people" to a relationship with Him. Prayer gives all people access to God. The wonderful plan of God was presented by Paul, "But as it is written: What no eye has seen and no ear has heard, and what has never come into a man's heart, is what God has prepared for those who love Him" (1 Cor. 2:9).

The priest or preacher has no more access to God than the child who believes in Christ. People who pray enter into God's presence. No matter what tongue, tribe, or nation is represented, people are special to Him. God desires relational conversations with all people.

Religious people in the temple episode enraged Jesus because they were blocking the space reserved for Gentiles to pray. The result was the temple became an exclusive place for a few "chosen" ones to enjoy God. The desire of God, before the foundation of the world that He "so loved," was for all peoples to know and experience Him.

How assuring are the words of God for all people groups! Jesus made reference to the Isaiah passage in Matthew that described the purpose of "His house." "And the foreigners who convert to the LORD, minister to Him, love the LORD's name, and are His servants, all who keep the Sabbath without desecrating it, and who hold firmly to My covenant—I will bring them to My holy mountain and let them rejoice in My house of prayer. Their burnt offerings and sacrifices will be acceptable on My altar, for My house will be called a house of prayer for all nations" (Isa. 56:6–7). Jesus was angry because prayer was relegated to a low/no priority position, particularly for those who were not "insiders."

TCs are places where prayer is taught as the way for everyone to connect with the one true God. Prayer is a priority because connecting with God is more important than connecting to programs.

3. *The response to His praying people.* Why is prayer important for His people to engage? Why is prayer the purpose of His house? Because prayer is a relationship and conversation with God. Jesus invites people to invite Him into their lives and circumstances through praying. Jesus gives people the resource and capability to affect the lives of other people. People who pray enjoy a deeper level of partnership with God to change the world because they take time to follow His leadership.

James described the significance of prayer, "Therefore, confess your sins to one another and pray for one another, so that you may be healed. The intense prayer of the righteous is very powerful. Elijah was a man with a nature like ours; yet he prayed earnestly that it would not rain, and for three years and six months it did not rain on the land. Then he prayed again, and the sky gave rain and the land produced its fruit" (James 5:16–18). Prayer is significant because prayer is powerful. Its power is found in the God to whom we pray. His desire for us is to invite Him into events of our lives so we can be a partner with the King. The Lord wants to involve us in His divine work.

> *Praying in His will with the right heart will make a difference in the affairs of the world.*

Do you ever wonder why God would invite us to pray? Isn't God going to do what God is going to do? In certain matters, yes, God is going to do what God is going to do. But the mystery of prayer alongside the sovereignty of God is the reassurance in this passage (and many others) that ascribe power and results in praying. God has chosen prayer to be a vehicle by which He changes people and the world. Praying in His will with the right heart will make a difference in the affairs of the world.

TCs have watched lives change after they prayed. From prayer in the past, they received leadership from the Spirit for their church. They pray expectantly that God will continue to respond to their requests for guidance, empowerment, and change in their community.

Transformational Prayer Practices

TCs in our study valued and practiced prayer. They embraced the values of Jesus. Different methods and traditions influence the act of praying in Transformational Churches. What does a church deeply committed to prayer look like? Certain principles were consistent and valuable to consider.

1. Praying churches experience breakthroughs. Churches with transformational practices varied in size, location, methods, and denomination. But churches that experienced any type of breakthrough or turnaround highlighted prayer in their story. "Pastors and churches have to get uncomfortable enough to say, 'We are not New Testament Christians if we don't have a prayer life.' This conviction makes us squirm a little, but how else will there be a breakthrough with God."[4]

For many churches prayer has been and will be the place of a cathartic experience. The recognition that many members regard prayer as unimportant will cause leaders and/or the members to feel conviction. It might even cause sorrow and anger, as in the life of Jesus. No matter the emotional reaction, acknowledging the lack of prayerful dependence may well become the cathartic experience necessary for a church to enter the Transformational Loop.

Pastor Randall Smith of Vista Hills Church, El Paso, Texas, experienced a breakthrough initiated through prayer. Prayer teams began praying every night at the church facility. Prayers were focused on preparing people for the coming of Jesus. They were not necessarily looking toward the end of the age. The question that informed their praying was, "What would it look like for people to be prepared for God to move into the midst of their church in whatever fashion He chose?" For three years and counting the people of Vista Hills Church have met and prayed every day for at least an hour. They pray for church leaders, direction of the church, and families in the church.

Pastor Smith believes the result of praying has been transformational. The entire culture of the church has been changed. The prayer for preparation to Pastor Smith meant that God would change them into "people like David, after God's own heart, a people that could hear the Lord and respond quickly, people who would be faithful to the Lord, . . . and He has answered that prayer." Vista Hills Church has become a church that prays through every detail of their organization. Church positions are filled through prayer. Pastor Smith goes to his prayer team with every dilemma and concern he faces. "The prayer team is the end," said Pastor Smith, "If this is a giant ship, . . . that prayer team is the engine room. It is everything."

Christ United Methodist Church in Fairview, Illinois, (Metro St. Louis) was plateaued in the 1990s. Pastor Shane Bishop believed something changed in 2001. The church relocated in the late '90s but in 2001 the church "just took off." People at Christ Church embraced a deeper practice of prayer. Currently one of the prayer teams gathers on Sunday mornings before church. The team walks through every area in the church facilities where activities will take place. They pray for the pastors and the worship leaders. "For me," Pastor Bishop said, "prayer is absolutely foundational." He continued, "Prayer plants dynamite, and evangelism detonates the dynamite. If you don't have the dynamite planted, there's nothing to detonate. So prayer, I believe, is absolutely essential."

As we wrote in chapter 2, any of the transformational practices can be the place where a church experiences breakthrough. Prayer, however, seemed to permeate all of the scenarios we studied. TCs were consistently places where prayer played a role in all they did. Whether engaging in their specific mission assigned by God or connecting through intentional relationships, prayer was vital to witnessing spiritual breakthroughs.

2. Praying churches have praying leaders. The principle of modeling is a recurring theme in TCs. Whether engaging the community, embracing relationships with lost people, or praying, pastors of TCs embody the practices embraced by the New Testament church. Their first calling is to live like Christ. Their second calling is to equip the saints through being an Ephesians 4 pastor-teacher.

Pastor Travis Adams of Mountain Presbyterian Church in Blairsville, Georgia, prays for people in his congregation every day using a church directory. Pastor Wayne Jenkins of South Run Baptist Church of Springfield, Virginia, "practices what he preaches" in personal prayer. He said, "Ever since I got here, I wanted South Run to be more of a prayerful church. The only way that was going to happen is if I became more prayerful too." Pastor Jenkins has morning, noon, and evening prayer times. In addition to personal worship during these times, he prays for the congregation by name. He also prays over the pews and through Sunday School rooms.

> *Whether engaging in their specific mission assigned by God or connecting through intentional relationships, prayer was vital to witnessing spiritual breakthroughs.*

3. *Praying churches commonly experience answers to prayer.* Prayer environments are marked by God's intervention. Stories of answered prayer are celebrated. God is glorified when answers to prayer are undeniable. Transformational leaders know stories are critical to fuel prayer movements in their churches.

Pastor John Lawrence of Lake United Methodist Church in Chippewa Lake, Ohio, said, "It starts with me. . . . I often speak of amazing answers and power that I have experienced in prayer." Pastor Thomas Wright of Memorial Baptist Church in Columbus, Ohio, believes the stories of answered prayer are critical to the establishment of a strong praying environment. One of the most exciting things for Pastor Wright is to see the fruit of praying. He said the stories do not have to be big, but they are significant when people hear what God is doing in response to praying. "To me," Pastor Wright said, "fruit from prayer is just great."

Unfortunately many believers pray without any substantive belief, as if we believe more in the tacked-on "if it be thy will" caveat than in the God to whom we pray. TCs pray because they believe it matters that they pray. For your church to become a Transformational Church, it must believe that God answers the prayers of His people.

4. Praying churches pray for members by name. TCs have great confidence in their ability to make a difference in the lives of others by praying for them. Paul demonstrated a life committed to praying for other believers. He told the Ephesian Christians, "This is why, since I heard about your faith in the Lord Jesus and your love for all the saints, I never stop giving thanks for you as I remember you in my prayers" (Eph. 1:15–16)

Macedonia United Methodist Church in Alpharetta, Georgia, practices praying for attendees by name. Pastor Sam Newman called prayer "the most important facet of our church, period." Pastor Newman stated the value, and the church has demonstrated the behavior to verify the value. Every Sunday at noon people gather at this church to "pray the pews." A designated person gathers the registration pad from each pew. Every person who attends services signs the pew register. The pads are placed on the altar. People join together there, kneel, and pray for each person who signed the register. Pastor Newman believes the public prayer experience for his people is critical to their personal growth in praying. "We try to make the focal point of prayer to be like tasting honey . . . tasting a relationship with God."

> **People learn to pray by praying.**

Mountain Presbyterian Church in Blairsville, Georgia, has prayer chains and prayer groups like most churches. However, they have a unique system to pray for their membership. Every year all members are randomly assigned to other members and informed of their assignments. They are asked to pray every day on behalf of the person to whom they are assigned. Members often send cards reminding others of their commitment to pray for them.

5. Praying churches have systems and processes. Most of the examples of praying in churches are tied into something tangible that keeps prayer happening. Prayer as with most priorities in a local church rarely happens all by itself. People will never grow deeper in prayer unless something is consistently placed in front of them to teach and remind. Resources and support systems are important parts of prayer in TCs. People are always learning how to pray and, thus, go deeper in prayer. New believers are often taught the basics of prayer in discipleship classes. But no question, people learn to pray by praying. Churches offer people simple systems to help them engage prayer on a more frequent and deeper level.

Macedonia United Methodist Church has a prayer system started by a woman in their church. Forty-five families are ready to pray in an instant through e-mail contact. Pastor Newman notifies the leader who will have people praying within fifteen minutes of his contact.

Trinity Church of God in Columbus, Ohio, has a visual system to help people practice and request prayer. Pastor Kenneth King has a preservice prayer area. Pastor King had the church take a visual overflow area to create an "upper room." A large wall hanging is included where people can attach prayer requests. People spend time at the "wall of prayer" praying in the upper room. Prayer inserts are in the weekly bulletin at Trinity. Requests are on one side of the insert. On the other side is a daily prayer chart asking them to pray for something different each day. The prayer guides are redistributed for the midweek meeting and used to guide corporate prayer times.

Pastor Wayne Jenkins of South Run Baptist Church in Springfield, Virginia, came back from sabbatical with a new commitment to prayer. Disappointment in his people's interest in prayer inspired more intentional approaches to help them grow. He started a daily prayer blog that included Scripture and prayer for every day. His desire for his people is to "draw them to prayer and worship wherever they are."

Though prayer occurs spontaneously throughout a TC, having a process for its growth and expansion is seen as important for making disciples. The difference between a TC and other churches is that the process to encourage prayer is subservient to prayer itself. Churches that have not yet made it to a transformational level often allow the program intended to encourage prayerfulness to become the priority over prayer itself. A classic example is the traditional Wednesday night prayer meeting. In the vast majority of these meetings, the hour-long service is dominated by reading a prayer request list and Bible teaching from the pastor. Both of those activities are important but normally the least amount of time of the service is given to actual prayer. And then it is normally voiced by the pastor or another key leader.

TCs have developed programs that encourage all believers to learn more about prayer and to pray with greater frequency. Rather than relying on the professional clergy of the church, in a TC the members find great satisfaction in becoming personally active in prayer.

6. *Praying churches value corporate prayer.* Prayer is about a relationship in Transformational Churches. Many pastors in our research consistently taught from the pulpit about prayer. Also, they clarified that prayer was not a religious duty but a relationship born out of love for God. They clarified the multiple aspects of prayer beyond intercession.

Pastor Thomas Wright has taught his membership in Columbus, Ohio, to learn to accept the fact that sometimes their prayers are not answered the way they prefer. "One of the phrases our people use around here is, 'it's not about us; it's about Him.'"

Lake United Methodist Church in Chippewa Lake, Ohio, places a high value on public prayer. Pastor John Lawrence describes their public prayer as "honest" and "powerful." "We stress that in our church these are holy moments when we pray together as a congregation . . . almost as if we are standing in awe of God whose presence we are in." Pastor Lawrence further described the powerful statement affirmed as they pray together, "We are acknowledging corporately as a family of God . . . we have experienced great answers to prayer in the past, and we expect to see those answers again this time and future times."

TCs desire to witness God's move to transform the entire community around them. They hope to see Him change everyone who attends the church. Because they hope for so much from God, they are eager to pray about it together. Relational intentionality converged with prayerful dependence again and again throughout our study.

Transformational Churches want to pray together. Praying together is consistent with a deep desire to see lives and their community transformed by the power of Christ. They enjoy the community interaction with God. They grow close to one another through hearing the church petition for God's work together. Churches that pray together see God's work together.

7. *Praying churches engage their communities through prayer.* As we wrote earlier, prayer is a response to God's character and heart. Churches that regularly display their dependence on God through prayer are more likely to act according to His heart and join Him in His work. Prayerfulness should lead to a greater desire to act. If it does not, then you are doing it wrong.

Pastor Rob Watts leads the membership of West Columbus Church of God in Columbus, Ohio, to engage neighborhoods through prayer. He recently led them to take nine-volt batteries door-to-door offering to change out the batteries in their neighbor's smoke detectors. As they left, they asked their neighbors if they had anything they could pray about. They reach out to their community one Sunday a month and asked each person contacted for prayer requests.

First Baptist Church of Carrizo Springs, Texas, engages their community through prayer walking. Pastor Robert Krause personally leads his church to prayer walk neighborhoods. By doing so, they have numerous conversations with people who are curious about what they are doing.

Pastor Mark Britton of Hitchcock United Methodist Church in Hitchock, South Dakota, meets each Saturday night with what he calls, "a community of the faithful." The prayer meeting includes people from his church and other churches in the community. The purpose of the meeting is to pray for community needs. The meeting has been going on for over a year. Pastor Britton believes the prayer meeting has been used of God for many purposes. People have experienced the power of God and seen amazing answers to prayer since beginning "the community of the

> *Prayerfulness should lead to a greater desire to act. If it does not, then you are doing it wrong.*

faithful." Pastor Britton said when people in the community know they are being prayed for by "the community of the faithful" it brings joy to them, which he believes aids the healing process in peoples' lives.

David Garrison captured the desperation of God's people that moves them to pray for their communities:

> We pray because our vision exceeds our abilities. Prayer is the soul's deepest cry of rebellion against the way things are, seeing the lost of the world and crying out, 'This does not glorify God, and so, by God's grace, it must change!' Prayer comes from God and ascends back to God on behalf of those who do not know God.[5]

Prayer in the TCs follows the passion of churches for people in the harvest. Consistent with Jesus' heart for the harvest, the focus of prayer is not only for the sick or the members of a church but for the people who have yet come to know Him.

8. *Praying churches have big prayer events.* Transformational Churches practice ongoing prayer gatherings and other prayer processes. Prayer also includes "big event" venues. Vaughn Forest Baptist Church celebrated their fifteenth anniversary celebration with a prayer event. Each year they have the same event that dedicates a day of praying for each year the church has been in existence. More than six hundred people prayed for at least an hour for fifteen days. One of the valuable by-products of the event is that new attendees see a vivid demonstration of how important prayer is to the life of the church. Numbers are not necessarily the only scorecard for success, but Pastor Phipps believes they gauge the spiritual passion of his people.

Concord is a city of around sixty-six thousand people in northeast Charlotte, North Carolina. Prayer is a transformational practice for Pastor Leon Hawks and his three-year-old congregation. Sunday morning gatherings are highlighted by conversational prayers with specific purposes such as praise and petition prayer times. An "Embrace Prayer" box is located outside the worship center to provide an ongoing link between prayer and the needs of attendees.

Crosspointe is a prayer-walking and a prayer-driven church. "We do a lot of prayer walking here," said Pastor Hawks. From prayer walking over their new church property to "windshield tour" praying through their community, prayer has moved from a philosophy of ministry to a practice. "We'll go to lunch sometimes, and a community will come to mind that we have not reached. It's nothing unusual for us to go and park at the entrance and pray for the community," Pastor Hawks said. All-day prayer meetings take place twice a year at Crosspointe. The twelve hour prayer meetings begin at 6:00 a.m. Rooms in the church building are set up as prayer stations based on distinct needs. Participants move from room to room to invest a focused time of intercession based on each need. Prayer is the *engine* of Transformational Churches.

Prayer Environments in Transformational Churches

Prayer sounds like the Christian thing to do. Prayer is always the right answer to most questions that present a problem to be solved. But how many Christians and churches really pray? Our research supported the significance of a church that not only valued prayer but practiced prayer. When you find those churches, you will find Transformational Churches.

How did those churches get to the point of really praying? In those churches prayer was valued and practiced to the point of gaining momentum from God. Once people started experiencing the power and presence of God through prayer, more people started to catch on. Notice what our research revealed.

> *Our research supported the significance of a church that not only valued prayer but practiced prayer.*

- "Attending my church causes me to want to pray more in my personal life." (83 percent of TC members strongly or moderately agree)

Churches that cultivate environments that motivate people to pray could never do that through manipulation or expectations. Church environments that cause people to pray consistently experience answers to prayer and practice praying.

Prayer leaders agree that we are missing our most significant resource when we neglect the spiritual discipline of prayer. We live in an age where we have so many other methods or activities to resort to besides prayer. We need prophetic voices to embrace the need of calling the church to prayer. Our pulpits have been multiplied through technology. Not only should the message be sent from our Sunday morning messengers but from our Web sites, books, and blogs. Our only hope is divine intervention, not our latest revitalization tool or church-planting strategies. Where people pray, God works. Where God works, transformation happens.

> *Where people pray, God works. Where God works, transformation happens.*

Leonard Ravenhill was born in England in 1907. He influenced many great leaders and churches through his writing, teaching, and preaching. His prophetic voice cried out for revival and spoke against prayerlessness. As we continue to be overwhelmed by lostness in North America and desperate for answers, we need more voices calling for prayer. Here is what Ravenhill said in his most famous book first published in 1959:

> Poverty-stricken as the church is today in many things, she is the most stricken here, in the place of prayer. We have many organizers, but few agonizers; many players and payers, few prayers; many singers, few clingers; lots of pastors, few wrestlers; many fears, few tears; much fashion, little passion; many interferers, few intercessors; many writers, but few fighters. Failing here, we fail everywhere.[6]

"Failing here we fail everywhere." We see little evidence that many of us believe that . . . yet. But when we run out of other options, we will. We hope it is not too late . . . then. Transformational Churches are already there.

Transformational Churches have a missionary mentality (Discern). They emphasize the three key values of vibrant leadership, relational intentionality, and prayerful dependence (Embrace). In the next three chapters we will see three primary manifestations of transformation in the part of the loop called Engage. The first of these is the experience of true worship, the subject of our next chapter.

7
Worship: Actively Embrace Jesus

For the LORD is great and is highly praised;
He is feared above all gods.

(1 Chronicles 16:25)

BY THE NUMBERS

We see evidence of God changing lives as a result of our worship services. (75 percent strongly or moderately agree)

Story of Success

Community Bible Church, San Antonio, Texas, has plenty of work to keep their worship teams busy. The congregation has ten off-campus venues and six on-campus services each week. Thousands of people participate. However, size and activity levels do not make CBC transformational.

CBC empowers people to do ministry. Their ministry of praise and worship touches the world, yet there is a high bar for the hundreds that are involved. Praise and worship is not a performance or music genre for CBC.

Worship is a lifestyle. According to Worship Ministry Pastor Ray Jones, the expectations of worship leaders at CBC are simple. First, worship leaders must worship. Leaders must experience authentic worship before they lead others. Second, worship teams must worship. Then Pastor Jones believes the congregation will follow. He compares worship leadership to parenting. "Like parenting you model the behaviors you want your children to imitate. Congregations learn to worship by watching their leaders worship," said Pastor Jones.

Worshippers at CBC lead outreach efforts. According to Pastor Jones, "Authentic worship always produces the experienced presence of God. People's lives are changed in His presence." Some of the most aggressive evangelistic efforts of CBC are led by worship leaders. San Antonio Juvenile Detention Center, inner-city housing, military bases, prisons, outdoor block parties, public amphitheaters, malls, and conventions are common venues for the CBC worship teams. Leaders experience personal transformation as they worship outside the walls of the church. God uses CBC worship teams as tools of transformation on campus and around the world. *Transformational Churches actively embrace Jesus through worship.*

TRANSFORMATIONAL LEADERS SPEAK . . .

"Worship anticipates not only an encounter with God, but also a clear next word from God. Worship is totally God-centered! God-focused! Out of worship comes a clearer and more focused relationship of faith and obedience with God. Worship is God's way of developing character and directing life into the center of His will."[1] —Henry Blackaby, *Created to Be God's Friend*

"We really see worship as a conversation or a time of community with God Himself as He speaks to them. He encourages us. Sometimes He challenges us, chastises us, inspires us; and we really see ourselves as a dynamic community of people that are formed by God Himself, God's words, the person of Christ. So we really seek to have that holy encounter, that communion with God in worship." —John Terpstra, Immanuel Christian Reformed Church, Fort Collins, Colorado

Worship–Engaging in the First Action

Worship is perhaps the most important action of the human experience. The human heart is designed to find someone or something to hold in highest esteem. God's intention from the beginning was to hold that esteemed position in our lives.

Transformational Churches place worship at the center point of their efforts. And for the moment we do not mean the sixty- to ninety-minute gathering on Sunday mornings. TCs cast their lot on the fact that God deserves to be worshipped. The motivation to see people of all nations become disciples of Christ is rooted in their desire to see God receive the honor He deserves. TCs have such a love for God that they know worship is a manner of living and not a mode of church programming.

> *Transformational Churches actively embrace Jesus through worship.*

But for the purposes of our study, we needed to discover both the attitudes and activities where transformation took place. The worship gathering or service is the most common activity of the vast majority of churches. Worship services are held by growing, plateaued, and declining churches. Churches of every denomination, type, and theological perspective have worship services. And all of them hold to the underlying idea that God deserves to be worshipped.

But churches that qualify as a Transformational Church are those where merely scheduling and holding a worship service are not enough. They have a high confidence that lives will be impacted through worship because their worship expressions consistently present the truth of who Jesus is and what He desires for the lives of people. Their services are alive with anticipation.

A sense of anticipation permeates Transformational Churches. In mission work they expect lives to be changed. In community they expect people to connect. In evangelism they expect disciples to be made. The same sense of anticipation charges their worship services with an enthusiasm that differentiates them from other churches.

In our study, we put this statement in front of churches:

- "A sense of anticipation and expectancy surrounds our worship services." (70 percent of TC members strongly or moderately agree)

> *TCs have such a love for God that they know worship is a manner of living and not a mode of church programming.*

In TCs people gather with the expectation that something amazing will happen. In many churches—too many churches—the leaders and people gather without such anticipation. They have grown accustomed to the service (as the old joke goes) beginning at 11:00 sharp and ending at 12:00 dull. In a TC the people arrive with expectancy and leave with excitement.

Two other statements in our survey further our insight into the life of a TC.

- "We see evidence of God changing lives as a result of our worship services." (75 percent strongly or moderately agree)
- "People regularly make decisions to obey God as a result of our worship services." (67 percent strongly or moderately agree)

Worship at a TC focuses on more than a mystical presence of God. Because of an intentional emphasis on presenting the claims of Christ and His Word, a TC expects God's presence to be real and transformative in their worship experiences. Knowing this, they look for and ask for people to change because of God's gift of mercy.

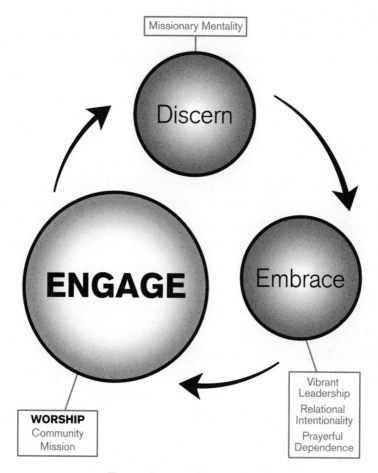

Transformational Loop

Corporate Gathering Matters

Taking issue with the corporate gatherings of God's people is in vogue. Many people report that worship numbers are sliding at an alarming rate. David T. Olson predicted that by 2020 only 14.7 percent of the North American population will be in a Protestant or Catholic worship gathering on any given Sunday.[2] Researcher George Barna shocked the Christian world when he predicted that the church would decline in weekly attendance another 50 percent by 2025. He predicted the trend of "mini-movements" would continue to grow. In the "mini-movements" Christ followers will become more nomadic, randomly moving from events, to groups, to experiences to support their relationship with God. Others would make the most biblical form of church the small informal groups of people who experience God in the comfort of their own homes.[3] Some believe that the organized large Sunday worship gathering in a centralized location will morph into organic house churches.

We see some benefits to the house church movement, particularly when the purpose is to create missional safe zones for the unchurched, dechurched, and never churched to find and follow God. We affirm much of the movement. But some of the angst against churches that have a structured weekly approach is unfounded. The crowds and the core (small-group structures) are both needed. After all, the church was born from the gathering of a large crowd when three thousand were saved. God's first church planting strategy was from crowd to core.

The crowd and the core are complementary elements God uses for His purposes. Turning crowd (big gathering) or core (small groups) into a methodological argument is just another way Satan divides and distracts from the real mission of God. TCs anticipate life change in both larger and smaller gatherings. Temple worship and house gatherings by believers in the first generation of the church resulted in life transformation because they shared the essential components of worship—the revelation of Jesus, the power of the Holy Spirit, and the bride of Christ responding in surrender and adoration.

Reasons for Corporate Gatherings

The results of the corporate gatherings bring us back to the main focus of this chapter. *First, God is glorified when Christians gather together to worship Him.* Groups of believers should gather to lift up the name of God and celebrate His work. It will cause those who pass by to ask, "Why?" Then we can say, "Because God is the only One worthy of such adoration and surrender."

A second result of corporate gatherings is that people will look over our shoulders to the God of our experience. People will witness our worship and ask, "Who?" Worship draws attention to the One we worship.

Third, our worship provides a defense for the faith that is not man-made but is God authored and supernatural. People will witness our worship and ask, "Where? Where did all of this come from?" Worship gatherings are a "not about me" experience. We don't gather trying to impress crowds with our technology, innovation, and creativity but to passionately worship the God who saves.

Worship is both an experience and a healthy lifestyle for believers. It reminds us of God's reign in our own lives and serves as a sign of His holiness to those outside the faith.

What Happens When We Gather?

We value—as do Transformational Churches—the weekly large gathering of God's people. But not as an achievement in and of itself. The traditional question at the Monday pastors' meeting of, "How many you runnin'?" is not the *only* relevant metric. Making attendance of worship gatherings a measure of success seems unavoidable. We should want more people to attend worship because it is a signal of priority. Attendance should lead to something greater in the life of a worshipper.

The first Sunday morning scorecard question is, How many people attended our worship service? The follow-up question should be, How many encountered the transforming presence of God through worship? We need to invest in questions that focus our energies in the right place. What God does in the lives of those who attend becomes the priority.

> *We don't gather trying to impress crowds with our technology, innovation, and creativity but to passionately worship the God who saves.*

Yes, there is something to be said for a family who gets three children dressed and attends church on Sunday morning, a single adult who attends church on her own, a senior adult couple with health challenges who brave a cold winter morning to worship. But the big question is, What happens when they get there? Are we creating consumers of religious goods and services or making disciples? Corporate gatherings should push people beyond mere observation of religious activities to an experience with the gospel. When people attend worship, are they simply observing a show or being transformed by God?

The questions TCs ask about worship gatherings are different—and more substantive—than most churches ask.

Sally Morganthaler explained the perspective of a worship leader/planner approach to Sunday:

> As a worship planner, I still ask myself the question, How are people going to encounter God in this time of worship? But increasingly, I'm focusing on the God of our experience, not the experience itself. The reason for this is that it's entirely possible to feel close to God without really focusing on who He is. It's entirely possible to work ourselves into worship euphoria without distinguishing between god generic and God incarnate. And in this age of spiritual pluralism, that difference is pivotal. . . . Worship leaders: Do we lead people into the throne room of a generic god, or do we draw them into the presence of the One, revealed and made eternally accessible to us in Jesus Christ?[4]

Most churches read the quote above and reply with: "Hopefully we do this most of the time." Transformational Churches read such a quote, and their reply is: "Of course. What else would we do?" The TC plans on seeing people drawn in before God's presence, experience His power, and be transformed by His grace.

Connecting Transformational Worship and the Mission of God

Worship is not a compartmentalized part of our Christian life in the generic file drawer of spiritual disciplines. Worship serves to connect us with Christ and equip us for ministry. Little of substance will be done in the name of a God we have never experienced. True worship allows us to experience God at a deeper level. When you experience God on a deeper level, personal and corporate mission will always follow.

The prophet Isaiah had a transformational experience in the presence of God. He was depressed with his life. The people he was called to help were failing on every level—socially, morally, and spiritually. A king suffered the judgment of God and died because of his spiritual failings. Isaiah entered God's presence with grief and disappointment. But God made an appearance that would prove to revive the prophet for future effectiveness.

When Isaiah saw the vision of God on the throne, it reminded him of God's authority and ability. Arriving depressed, Isaiah left transformed because God is always able to change our circumstances. But no matter the negative in Isaiah's life, the throne room was a positive experience. God accomplishes the unusual and unexplainable when we worship. Those who experience His presence know His presence is real, not man-made.

God had an agenda in the life of Isaiah. As Isaiah recognized God's presence, embarrassment set in on the prophet. God's holiness uncovers us. As His holiness is revealed, we better recognize our sin. And it is God's design for this to occur.

> *God accomplishes the unusual and unexplainable when we worship.*

In God's presence Isaiah was confronted with his own sin. The prophet's humiliation and confession in the divine throne room was necessary. God's transformation of Isaiah is a beautiful picture of the gospel. "Then one of the seraphim flew to me, and in his hand was a glowing coal that he had taken from the altar with tongs. He touched my mouth [with it] and said: 'Now that this has touched your lips, your wickedness is removed, and your sin is atoned for'" (Isa. 6:6–7).

The word for atonement here is "Yom Kippur" or the day of covering. Yom Kippur is a special holiday in the Jewish faith that acknowledges God's provision of forgiveness of sin. The twenty-four-hour celebration commemorates the forgiveness God provided to the children of Israel after they worshipped the golden calf in the wilderness. It does not mean that God overlooks sin, but that He pays the cost for it. It is a transformational truth.

Real worship will transform the worshipper. Transformed worshippers will change the world. God asked Isaiah two questions. "Then I heard the voice of the Lord saying: 'Who should I send? Who will go for Us?' I said, 'Here I am. Send me'" (Isa. 6:8).

For Isaiah, real worship produced transformation. In church today transformed worshippers join the mission of God to change the world. Isaiah became one of those "sent" ones. So has every believer. Transformation by the gospel results in a sent life. As you gather a group of "sent ones," they have the opportunity to become a Transformational Church.

The Way Worship Looks: Reverence versus Relevance

Before we continue our consideration of transformational worship, a question must be resolved. It is, Does how we worship really matter? Put simply, yes. Are we seeking an experience with God or giving to God what He deserves? J. Oswald Sanders described the act of worship this way, "In the act of worship God communicates His presence to His people."

Jesus assured us, "For where two or three are gathered together in My name, I am there among them" (Matt. 18:20). He is already there, but as we worship, we engage the God who is already there. Sanders continued, "The word 'worship' derives from a word meaning 'to prostrate oneself, to bow down.' It is used of a dog fawning before its master. As we use it, it is 'the act of paying reverence and honor to God.'"[5]

Worship is the volitional act of our engaging and speaking publicly about the work of God. Worship is not music but includes it. Style does not determine the message of Christ. Worship is a matter of the heart. Paul wrote to the Colossians, "Let the message about the Messiah dwell richly among you, teaching and admonishing one another in all wisdom, and singing psalms, hymns, and spiritual songs, with gratitude in your hearts to

God" (Col. 1:16). When worship becomes an issue of style instead of heart, then there is a problem.

Worship should begin with the goal of clearly presenting the truth of Jesus. When the message of the Christ is communicated, then the church can admonish one another to live lives worthy of the gospel. By worshipping in truth and grace with one another, then we will see true expressions of praise of all kinds, including what we have sung in our traditions as well as the new expressions of worship and spontaneous expressions led by the Spirit. Reducing worship to a focus on style removes God as the reason for gathering.

At Vaughn Forest Baptist Church, Pastor Lawrence Phipps has led his congregation to have three identical worship services because he believes worship is not a matter of style but focus. Pastor Phipps said, "If our focus is people, then let's have three kinds of services, but if our focus is the Lord, then let's lead our people to focus on Him. They won't be sitting there thinking about music styles."

The way we worship is causing a stir in the body of Christ these days. Yet the emotionally charged issue has always been controversial in the Christian movement. Contemporary or traditional? Praise team or choir? Guitar or organ? Dance? Drama? Christians and churches are divided over the right and wrong way to enjoy the presence of the Lord in worship. Who is right? Who is wrong?

One thing that sets churches apart as TCs is that they do not become bogged down in false dichotomies of ministry. The false comparison between relevance and reverence is an illustration of such. But because the conversation is so prevalent, we feel the need to address it here.

Many churches where worship has grown cold or disengaging try to liven it up with a change of music style. Such a tactic normally leads to conflict because we choose to emphasize man-centered preferences. Focusing instead on the clear revelation of God and the authority of His Word will lead to the liberty brought by the Spirit.

Will the way we worship be a controversy we can overcome? Yes and no. Yes, we will finally overcome the controversy but not until we reign with Jesus forever in the new Jerusalem (Rev. 21). In the Holy City there will be many no more death, crying, pain, temple, sun, moon, closed gates, or night according to Revelation 21. We can reasonably hope that there will be no more debates about musical styles as we worship God forever. Jesus will be the focus, not the way we worship! The attitudes of angry senior adults or bored twenty-somethings will pass away! But back to the here and now—no, as long as there are people, preferences, and our sin nature, there can be division about the way we worship.

Controversy about music styles has existed since the early history of the church. Ambrose (AD 390–347), bishop of Milan, was highly influential on hymn singing in Western churches and is considered "the Father of Latin Hymnody." In fact, Ambrose introduced a new style of singing that was easier for commoners to sing and that appealed to the emotions. Yet his critics did not appreciate his new approach.

> *Reducing worship to a focus on style removes God as the reason for gathering.*

All types of controversy emerged when Handel presented his famous and revered *Messiah*. Typical to Handel's writing style, a lot of the melodies he employed in *Messiah* had been used in his operettas that were off-Broadway type productions. The first ten times Messiah was presented, Handel was considered a heretic by many. He was criticized for performing the music in secular venues and using secular music behind the sacred words.

Throughout history the church has fought over music. From Gregorian chants to Handel's *Messiah* to Larry Norman ("Why Should the Devil Have All the Good Music?"), we battle over the personal, emotional issue of music choices. People embrace their style of music with great passion. The concession that there will always be worship wars may be disheartening. The mission of the devil is to keep lost people lost. Distracting us from the glory of God is an ingenious strategy. When music is confused with worship, Satan wins. The desire for transformation is replaced with a desire for musical taste. It's a poor trade-off.

Every generation dislikes the previous generation's music. And many in each generation also dislike the next generation's music. So there is a constant tension between three generations about their preferences between at least three kinds of music. We fight about musical style, yet God uses all kinds of music for His glory and honor. We are fighting over cultural forms when we should engage in biblical meanings. Can God use different forms of music? Yes. Remember, worship is an issue of the heart. And from the biblical record, we find no such thing as Christian music, only Christian lyrics.

No matter your feelings about the *how* of worship, all of us agree that worship is biblical and, therefore, should be transformational. Transformational Churches in our study consider worship foundational to what they do. Their worship gatherings are a common front door or introduction to their church. Worship is also a critical vehicle for making disciples. So if there is a sweet spot for a Transformational Church, then worship plays a vital role.

Decisions must be made. Styles and methodologies must be chosen. So how does someone decide?

Current worship wars have two sides. One is driven by what is believed to be relevance. What kind of musical style will connect with the people we are trying to reach and encourage true worship? The other side is represented by those who feel that reverence is the key element for worship. The first group is trying to pull the church forward (from their perspective). The second is trying to push the church back to a more reverent style. The pushing and pulling is the problem. A right or wrong side does not exist. In most cases the pushers and the pullers have missed the point. Additionally both pushers and pullers are causing unnecessary division in the church and damage to the testimony of Christians. We should all remember that worship is as timeless as God.

How does the Bible inform us about reverence? Reverence is expressed by David through dancing. "David was dancing with all his might before the LORD wearing a linen ephod" (2 Sam. 6:14). David humbled himself as king and took on the position normally reserved for a slave who would lead a procession in the streets. His love for the Lord led to both an outburst of emotion and a celebratory dance.

Reverence in Revelation is expressed differently. John the apostle experienced the presence of the Lord in a powerful and awesome way. "When I saw Him, I fell at His feet like a dead man. He laid His right hand on me, and said, 'Don't be afraid! I am the First and the Last, and the Living One. I was dead, but look—I am alive forever and ever, and I hold the keys of death and Hades'" (Rev. 1:17–18). Two men of God, in the presence of the same God, experienced two different forms of reverence. One form was outward and animated; the other was lying still at the feet of Jesus.

Scripture must be our guide in these important decisions. Although there is plenty of room for different expressions in the presence of the Lord, note that there is plenty of permission too.

> "Be glad in the LORD and rejoice, you righteous ones; shout for joy, all you upright in heart." (Ps. 32:11)

> "Clap your hands, all you peoples; shout to God with a jubilant cry." (Ps. 47:1)

> "Praise Him with tambourine and dance; praise Him with flute and strings." (Ps. 151:4)

God is to be revered. The way we worship Him does matter. Most people who are calling for reverence, however, actually want to return to a preferred past, depending on their tradition. What reverence looks like differs from one culture to another. In Africa, I (Ed) have jumped with people in worship and bowed with others in Asia. Reverence is first an attitude of a heart, expressed and informed by the culture of the worshipper.

Commission or Conviction?

People on all sides of the worship issue have convictions that are actually personal preferences. Church leaders and planters often feel driven to offer worship as a guitar-driven, U2-style of contemporary worship. But just because it's on your iPod does not mean it is the contextually relevant way to worship. Leaders need to be careful to plan the worship service not in their heads but in their communities. Use the missionary mentality and discern the heart language of your community. Musical choices must be appropriate to the context.

No style of music is relevant to every culture in the world. Your current music style may match your community, but that could change in five years. Will you be willing to change, or will you insist on imposing your style of music on the people in the community you seem committed to reach? Pastor Lawrence Phipps does not like using words like *traditional* or *contemporary* to describe their worship. "We use a word here, we call it *relevant* worship. We talk about it is relevant worship for the time, which means that tomorrow that may change, and we have the freedom to do that." Music is the tool but will always change based on context. God never gave notes or melodies in Scripture. The Bible focuses on the outcomes of worship.

Often we insist that worship be the way it was when we grew up. Our musical preferences have deep roots. Your church involvement as a child and young adult may have been incredibly positive. But remember, it was God who spoke and God who worked in your life during those worship gatherings. The music was a vehicle through which God worked. God still works today through multiple music styles.

I (Ed) became a Christian in the 1970s. At that time the "7–11" music (seven words sung eleven times) was popular in Christian worship. I sang, "Do Lord, oh do Lord, oh do remember me." I learned worship in the late 1970s and early 1980s. I held my first church staff position when I was nineteen years old. I primarily worked with youth and I helped out a bit with the senior adults. Pretty interesting combination, don't you think?

One responsibility was to lead worship at a local nursing home. I remember my first visit. I was determined in all my wisdom to go teach those people how to really worship. Of course,

> *Use the missionary mentality and discern the heart language of your community.*

I brought the only legitimate worship instrument I knew, my guitar. I was ready to go show them a thing or two about worship. I remember a ninety-two-year-old lady, Mrs. Langley. She put her hand on my arm when I walked in and said, "Don't worry, we don't need that guitar. We are just going to sing, and we want you just to sing with us." We sang "The Old Rugged Cross," a song with which I had little familiarity. I watched those older saints of God. They worshipped and wept together. I left that place humbled. To think I believed a nineteen-year-old kid on a guitar was going to teach those saints of God how to worship. The challenge is to learn to be mature enough to worship in different ways.

A popular attempt to resolve the diversity of styles and musical tastes is to try a blend. Wouldn't a compromise make sense? Although it may make sense at first, we do not know of many examples of blended worship that resolved anything. God's purpose in worship is not to make everybody happy. God's desire is for people to discover and glorify Him through worship. Compromise is a dreadful word to use when we discuss worship.

Worship Pleasing to God

Jesus described God's desire for true worshippers in a conversation with a woman at a well in John 4. The woman came to the well with numerous issues including a string of broken relationships and a misunderstanding of worship. But Jesus did not avoid her. He brought up her relationship issues. She talked about locations. Jesus talked about life.

He taught her that the heart of worship is what matters most. "But an hour is coming, and is now here, when the true worshipers will worship the Father in spirit and truth. Yes, the Father wants such people to worship Him. God is spirit, and those who worship Him must worship in spirit and truth" (John 4:23–24). God longs for real worshippers.

Transformational Churches find a way for people to avoid the debates about place, style and method. They focus on maximum participation in worship. As Jesus taught, it must be at the levels of spirit and truth.

- "The majority of the people in our worship services actively participate." (66 percent strongly or moderately agree)

We all know that it is easy to anecdotally compare this to other churches. Without casting aspersions at your church (because we don't know it), we have been around the block a few times and know what most worship services are like.

If you are unsure, do this simple experiment. Sit somewhere different this Sunday, even if you are the leader of the church. Find a spot in the room where you can see most of the people gathered for worship and look to see if they are actively participating. Notice how many people are fully engaged as opposed to those who are passive. We hope you will be pleasantly surprised, but from our study we know most likely you will not. Accurate quantitative support is virtually impossible due to the "halo effect" of surveys but relatively easy to qualify the results. The halo effect tells us that people answer the way they think things should be rather than the way they actually are. We know from stories and testimonies that most people are not actively engaged during worship services.

Why does this happen? One contributing factor is the emergence of the "church artist." The church artist is a product of clergification where professionals do the work God intended for all believers. The artist is a gifted singer that approaches worship leadership as a performance of worship for others to enjoy as observers. It can inspire and connect with the audience and even at times engage the worshipper. In this approach, however, more often than not, the songs are too new, too vocally challenging, and the sound too aggressive to engage the average worshipper. Though appropriate for a concert, this approach creates passive worshippers. And passive worshippers usually live passive Christian lives.

TCs actively engage people in worship and are led by worship leaders who value participation over performance.

Reconciling Reverence and Relevance

If your bottom line is to please God in worship, then engaging in a war is futile. Too many people try to solve the impending or full-blown "worship war" with the indistinct blended service. Most agree that blended worship provides an equal opportunity to offend everybody. Why?

> *TCs actively engage people in worship and are led by worship leaders who value participation over performance.*

Foremost, to blend musical styles is often a carnal solution to a spiritual issue. Worship choices become all about me, my tastes, my preferences. It is a jukebox mentality of "I pay my money here and choose the songs I want to hear." Or it becomes an issue of bitter curiosity, "Why is my music not good enough for the young people and the people in our community?"

Blended is an exercise that is built on a wrong foundation: *What do I want? What do you want? How do we negotiate a truce?* Neither side is truly happy with a truce. A faulty assumption drives any truce—that worship style choices are the spiritual issue. Meanwhile, the God who should be worshipped is pushed aside as people argue over song selection. Worship must never be about me but about God and His glory.

The Purpose of Worship

As worship leaders embrace the heart of God, the focus will move from style to purpose: a desire for people to become true worshippers. The result will be new values. New values will then influence musical style and worship priorities. Keep in mind the value will not be to "keep everybody happy." Worship should be what unifies the body of Christ. Focusing on purpose will require certain principles at work in the church.

In corporate gatherings, we are not called to lead worship but to lead people into the presence of God. Our goals are spiritual. As our friend Mike Harland has said, "You will never achieve spiritual goals with a musical means." No style out there will enable you to achieve something spiritual.

Music is a tool. Music is only one aspect of worship. Worship is the goal. God is not about ritual or methods. He is about relationship.

Worship is a spiritual discipline that communicates a biblical meaning in a cultural form. Did you ever wonder what musical style God prefers? He doesn't. He calls people to worship Him in spirit and truth. The question driving us should be: What will God use here in this place in this time? TCs determine worship style based on biblical mandates about worship in principle and appropriate to their cultural setting in style. We must decide that it is not about our preferences. Paul described how Christianity is lived out in any context, "And He died for all so that those who live should no longer live for themselves, but for the One who died for them and was raised" (2 Cor. 5:15). Like the rest of the Christian life, the act of worship is done out of and for transformation.

Worship from your unity and choose music out of your mission. Worship unifies. Music rarely does. A church seeking the transformation of a community of far-from-God people must make their worship about God and His glory rather than their preferential styles. If we demand things in worship that cannot be demanded in every expression of church anywhere in the world, then we are demanding cultural elements not biblical elements.

Unhelpful voices in the church say you don't need to worry; the church is for believers. Teach them, and they will go out and reach the world. Churches like these tend not to reach many people. They look more like a chaplaincy (or hospice) than they do a place of life transformation. We think these voices have forgotten that we were all at one time not in the church.

When worship forms are chosen according to the mission, unbelievers say, "I see people who are encountering God, and they are like me." We must be careful not to let our worship style create artificial barriers to God. As we rethink the purpose of worship as opposed to worship style, we need to ask better questions. A better question is, How can worship be planned to lead people in this time and place to worship an eternal God? Another good question is, How can our worship be planned so people can focus on God and give Him praise, glory, and honor?

Research confirms the fact that growing churches tend to be more contemporary in worship style than traditional. There are exceptions. I (Ed) remember visiting my friend Tim Keller's Redeemer Presbyterian Church in Manhattan. You will witness thousands of twenty-somethings in a traditional worship service. The morning worship service is described as "classical." The evening worship service is a mixture of jazz and contemporary.

Redeemer Church describes their approach to worship:

> The Scriptures are filled with instruction to sing praise to God.
> Even Jesus sang hymns with his disciples. Redeemer includes
> the singing of psalms, hymns and spiritual songs (Eph. 5:19;
> Col. 3:16) at nearly every gathering—from worship services to
> leadership meetings, retreats and fellowship groups. . . . In fact,
> artistic expression is such an important part of everyday life that
> God commands us all to engage in it, whether as professionals
> or amateurs, and to do so with joy (Let the nations be glad and
> sing for joy! Psalm 67:4), originality (Sing to the Lord a new song.
> Psalm 96:1), and intellect (I will sing with my spirit, but I will also
> sing with my mind. 1 Cor. 14:15).[6]

Churches seeking the transformation of their community don't argue about music, but they are deeply concerned that worship occurs.

Worship is to be understood by those in need of transformation. Here's a question: Could a person far from Christ come into your worship service and see people like them in a worship context that makes sense to them? We are not talking about "seeker sensitive" or "seeker friendly" but "seeker comprehensible." Take into account when you plan worship that company will be there. Do not plan everything around them, but keep them in mind as you plan.

> *Like the rest of the Christian life, the act of worship is done out of and for transformation.*

More than anything, company needs to see Christians truly knowing and experiencing God through worship. To try to reduce the wonderful experience of God's presence to a method misses the point. We deliver the story of Jesus—who He is and what He has done for us—every time we worship Him. Paul described the be and do of the Christian worshipper, "Let the message about the Messiah dwell richly among you, teaching and admonishing one another in all wisdom, and singing psalms, hymns, and spiritual songs, with gratitude in your hearts to God" (Col. 3:16). The message of the Messiah should always be "seeker comprehensible."

Multiple Services in One Location?

Another attempt to resolve the worship wars is to provide multiple worship style options through multiple services. We support the desire behind multiple services. But a church holding multiple services in multiple styles must address the same concerns as if they were trying to blend it all in one place. What are the underlying motivations? If there is a desire to reach people or a mission-focused motivation, the consideration is healthy. The challenge might be for your congregation to move out of their church "comfort zone" to speak the language of people in your community who need Christ.

If you are driven by the desire to make people happy so they will not leave your church, then multiple services, multiple styles will not work. Multiples services and styles simply for the cause of numerical growth is not enough. To reach more churched people with multiple styles will ultimately cause disharmony in the larger body of Christ and damage other churches.

As new services are marketed, be careful not to announce to your community a "better way to enjoy church" or "this is not your father's church." Be cautious about pandering to the consumer needs of Christians inside or outside your church. Culture and language can be diverse within ministry areas of local churches and dictate a legitimate need for something different. However, if greater spiritual issues force the strategic decision, those issues will not be resolved. Multiple styles can cause resentment and greater division. Catering to religious consumerism can force a local church further down a disastrous road.

What if the decision to use multiple styles in multiple services has already been made by your church? What if the right motivation drove you and God led you? What can you do to ensure God will maximize the decision for His kingdom? *First, you should consistently, in all gatherings, reinforce the biblical values behind the decision.* Speak in terms of values, not styles. To say we believe guitar-driven worship is better than another style can be heard as a stylistic statement. A better discussion focuses on the value of experiencing the presence of God through public worship gatherings in a way people can understand best.

The second way to maximize multiple services with multiple styles is to promote other services during each service. Encourage people to visit each service for fellowship and unity. Highlight special testimonies of life change from one service to the next. For example, if a family comes to Christ that attended the traditional service, tell the story by video in the contemporary service. Share how each service is reinforcing the biblical values of experiencing God and reaching people.

A third way to maximize multiple services with multiple styles is to plan joint celebrations. Periodically gather the entire body together to celebrate the Christ who is not bound by musical styles. The service could feature multiple styles and testimonies from each service. Informal fellowship afterward might result in a greater appreciation for the mission of God and the body of Christ. Transformation will not happen in an environment of disharmony, so continually bring the church together to hear the stories of God's work among them all.

Addressing the Tough Worship Questions Together

We maintain that there will be no flawless solutions to the worship wars this side of heaven. Yet a healthy process of discerning God's will for your church can be transformational. Leaders and members should live humble lives of worship rather than focus on an hour-long event of worship. Live in the worship described in Scripture: "Therefore, through Him let us continually offer up to God a sacrifice of praise, that is, the fruit of our lips that confess His name" (Heb. 13:15). Address tough worship questions in a way that helps people embrace God's solutions by doing the following.

Ask the Lord. The issue is spiritual not musical. David was facing a critical issue and the future of a nation as he faced the Philistines. Not sure what strategic choices to make to win the battle, the Bible tells us he "inquired of God" (1 Chron. 14:10, 14). Though experienced in the battle since childhood, he asked God for wisdom. The best part of the story was not the part that David asked but that God answered in detail. Then David obeyed.

Prayerful dependence converges with our activity of worship. With so much at stake, engage the beauty of simple dependence on God for answers. He knows how He wants worship to look in your context. He cares about everyone involved in your church and who lives in your community.

Involve people. Transformational Churches let leaders lead. We stand by that position. But engaging people in prayer, Bible study, and dialogue can take a potentially divisive issue and change the outcome. When God enters the process, division can change to transformation.

God's will is not something that is decided by secret ballots in a church business conference. Remember what He said about sheep, "My sheep hear My voice, I know them, and they follow Me" (John 10:27). When engaging the dialogue, make worship issues a spiritual choice not a musical choice. Place the debate in spiritual terms not musical terms. The outcome might be a pleasant surprise. And you will model the values and process of discerning God's will in the matter.

> *Transformation will not happen in an environment of disharmony, so continually bring the church together to hear the stories of God's work among them all.*

Study Scripture. Seek to define the biblical values that will drive your worship decisions. Often the debate becomes emotional and self-centered. The conversation needs to revolve around the question, What does God want here and now? The journey to discover God's will should include careful study of His Word. Studying God's Word as a group over a specific direction on a specific matter (like worship for example) can be transformational.

Die to self. We might be guilty of "profiling," yet we have all experienced the same thing. We have walked into traditional churches in our suits and ties alongside teenagers and younger families. In turn we have walked into contemporary churches in our jeans and cool shirts with senior adults. Churches seeing transformation die to their preferences. Better yet, they are living in God's preference: to see the people in the community understand His revelation and submit to the Christ.

Avoid "truces." Sounds like strange advice, but truces often should be called "avoidances." Truces are temporary solutions to long-term issues. Instead, discover God's will through the intentional relationships shown in biblical community.

Study the community. Remember the first element we studied from the Transformational Loop? Missionary Mentality. And get ready for the last one: mission. We need to know: Who lives there? Whom has God called you to reach? What is the cultural, ethnic, or generational language of their heart? Music can be used by God to open the hearts of people, perhaps an entire community.

Ask new questions. The old question is, What kind of music do our people prefer? The new questions are: How can we lead people into the presence of God? How can we do what God has called us to do now, in this place in this time? What does the Bible value? Resource your worship leaders to learn and grow. Help them discover coaches and mentors.

Focus on revelation. Be intentional about spending more energy building worship experiences replete with the message about the Messiah than on the debate around stylistic preferences. In other words, spend more time on what you are doing than how you will do it.

> **Transformational Churches let leaders lead.**

Design new scorecards. Are people being changed through your public worship? Are they learning how to worship in a way that will carry over to their personal lives? Are they observing worship teams, and do leaders model genuine worship?

Conclusion

Mike Harland, author of *7 Words of Worship*, says it well: "Measure your worship not at 11 o'clock on Sunday morning but 8:30 on Monday morning in the cubicles where your people go to work." When lives have been reformed by the presence and power of God, then your worship is working.

Maybe your church has yet to experience conflict over music or worship styles. If your church is like most, eventually you will. Prepare by embracing values of biblical worship. Teach those values. When stylistic or methodological decisions are needed, decide on the basis of biblical values, not the preferences of the majority. And remember, if conflict surfaces in your congregation, embrace the conflict as an opportunity to learn two things. First, conflict can deepen your members' understanding of biblical worship. The question addressed should be, What does God's Word say about why and how we worship? Second, conflict can deepen your members' understanding of biblical conflict resolution. The question addressed should be, What does God's Word say about how the people of God should resolve conflict?

Jesus' prayer for future believers was that they would be one so that the world would believe in Him. "I pray not only for these, but also for those who believe in Me through their message. May they all be one, as You, Father, are in Me and I am in You. May they also be one in Us, so the world may believe You sent Me" (John 17:20–21). As passionate as we are about our style preferences in worship, there are more important issues at stake than winning. The world is watching. Men, women, and children are at stake. That we worship in unity and resolve disagreements in a Christlike manner is crucial to our mission to witness transformation in our communities.

Transformational Churches engage Jesus Christ in worship. They also engage the communities in which they live. We thus transition in the next chapter from connecting to God to connecting with people.

8

Community: Connect People with People

"For I want very much to see you, that I may impart to you some spiritual gift to strengthen you, that is, to be mutually encouraged by each other's faith, both yours and mine."
(Romans 1:11–12)

BY THE NUMBERS

New members are immediately taught about the importance of living in community with other Christians. (64 percent strongly or moderately agree)

TRANSFORMATIONAL LEADERS SPEAK

"The Bible defines what community is supposed to look like and how we as God's people are supposed to commit to and walk in relationship with one another. When a group of people obeys the Scriptures and walks in biblical community, at Midtown we call it a Life Group. Life Groups are our small groups. Life Groups

are the primary way people connect within the community of Midtown. Within Life Groups people pray together, worship together, eat together, laugh together, and serve together. We know and believe that there is a want inside all of us that desires to have real authentic relationships with others. We have discovered people finding this want meet through Life Groups."
—Dustin Willis, Midtown Fellowship, Columbia, South Carolina

"The early church made use of a very simple, very grassroots, very relational leadership development process: people investing in people. Although many churches and denominations claim to be using the structure of the early church, the only structure we can discern from the text are these face-to-face relationships between people."[1] —Bob Logan and Tara Miller, *From Followers to Leaders*

Life Together

Hey Adam,

I have a question. There is a girl in my Life Group right now that really wants to be in community. She is not able to get to Life Group or Midtown on Sunday nights because she is from Nigeria. She lives in Sandhills over thirty minutes away with no car. Our Life Group is selling some of our stuff in order to get a car for her so she can both get to LG and Midtown and to be able to go to work and to school. . . . I was wondering if we are able to get a car if Midtown could try to get a gas card for her for a little while.

Thanks,

Brittany

Brittany and her group are living out biblical community. This small group of college students from Midtown Fellowship in Columbia, South Carolina, goes beyond merely studying together. They do life together like the first generation of the church. In Acts 2 we get a remarkable picture of a robust relational church that in a lot of ways we've lost. The infant church had a challenge: How do we connect this many new converts to one another in significant relationships? We face a similar issue: How can we "assimilate" new Christians into the church? The church must have a process (organic and/or systematized) by which believers are connected to one another and growing in Christ. Today's church needs to experience a methodological regression to the early church of Acts 2.

The first church was truly organic. No seminars, no coaches, no consultants, but there seemed to be an intentional embrace of life after conversion both in corporate gatherings and smaller groups. They lived in a vibrancy of community.

Smaller groups were the lifeblood of the early church. Because life is an everyday occurrence, church should be as well. But in the North American church, we have shifted from the New Testament, relationship-driven community to a stage-driven community. The larger group, although vehemently defended by us in the previous chapter, does not function well as a stand-alone application of Christianity. How do we get back to the point where small communities matter?

When we use terms like *small groups* and *smaller communities*, we are referring to the system in your church where small groups of people gather for disciple making. For many churches (most in this study and, by extension, in North American churches), it is called Sunday School, where classes meet weekly on the church campus for study, encouragement, and evangelism. In other churches small groups meet in other places

> *Smaller groups were the life- blood of the early church.*

besides a church building for the same purposes. A growing number of churches use a hybrid of on- and off-campus groups. Whatever the name or method, the point of this transformational practice is that believers join their lives for the purpose of maturing in the faith and engaging in God's mission.

But we are not just talking about gathering in classes or groups. The local church is not in need of a new item on the menu of programs. We are not so much concerned with the container but with the fact that the church has become contained.

We believe that life change happens best among friends—both new and old. We call that small communities, but that can take different forms. Some people have pride or preference in one model or another, but we must let the research drive the data—and churches use many models. The Sunday School or small-group ministry of a church provides that environment. It is the ministry where accountability is built between believers. When we join our lives with honest relationships, we can better provoke one another to love and good deeds. The "flat" structure engages everyone to live on mission by encouraging maximum participation. Community is an activity that delivers transformation in people, churches, and communities.

> *We believe that life change happens best among friends— both new and old.*

Living in community with one another moves us away from a fortress mentality that creates a Christian subculture. Instead, it creates a "safe zone" where unbelievers feel comfortable asking hard questions and believers feel comfortable finding the encouragement they need for growing in the faith.

Community in a Transformational Church

Creating community and small-group Bible studies is critical for building a Transformational Church. Three of our survey questions shed light on the importance of small-group community in a TC.

- "Small groups are very important at our church." (77 percent strongly or moderately agree)
- "Our church regularly starts new small groups." (69 percent agree)
- "New members are immediately taught about the importance of living in community with other Christians." (64 percent strongly or moderately agree)

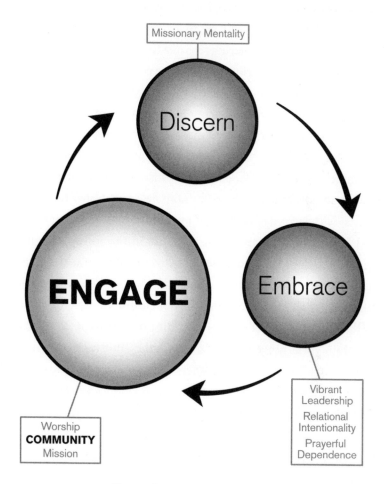

Transformational Loop

These results are significantly higher than other churches and show the centrality of connecting in small-group relationships to the life of a TC. We found that TCs put a premium on involving people in small-group communities within the congregation. This is so important that they place a heavy emphasis on getting new members immediately involved into small groups like Sunday School classes, home Bible study groups, and discipleship classes.

Beyond simply knowing that small groups are important to the effectiveness of a TC, we sought to discover the values that support them.

First, a smaller number of people provides a greater opportunity for personal discovery. By engaging in a small group or Sunday School class, the dynamic changes. Larger gatherings are like the showroom at your local car dealership. Tire kicking, curiosity, and value of life with Christ are put on display for the crowd to see. But if the large gathering is the showroom, then the small group is the service department where we look under the hood of our lives and explore faith in Christ more deeply. Dialogue replaces monologue. Tough questions about God, the Bible, and Jesus Christ are worked out in community. The smaller community also provides a platform to help others who are struggling. The community demonstrates how to merge Jesus Christ with everyday challenges by looking deeply into one another's lives and helping one another engage Christ in the most difficult times. Small-group relationships provide the environment for transformation.

Second, smaller communities are just that . . . communities. They are communities (small groups, Sunday School classes, house churches, work groups) through a variety of expressions. The program used to facilitate biblical community was not a deciding factor in the Transformational Church study. Some offer Sunday School. Others call them small groups, Bible fellowships, or classes. The common theme throughout our research is that TCs connect people to one another in relationships. Even with demographic diversity, people in small community find commonality in their desire to know Christ better. With their lives serving as the backdrop for the week-to-week narrative, they learn together how God connects to every aspect of their days. It is a journey that needs fellow travelers.

> **The program used to facilitate biblical community was not a deciding factor in the Transformational Church study.**

Finally, small groups are the best way to genuine life change through the local church. As we think about the definition of a small group, it is important to remember the goal—transformed lives. But just any group of people meeting together does not constitute a transformational small group. Six people meeting under a tree in the back of your shop at work is not necessarily a small group. Why would we state the obvious? Because relational intentionality is the key to transformational small groups. So whether the structure is a Sunday School church or a home-based small-group church, the reason TCs emphasize community is life transformation.

As we think about the definition of a small group, it is important to remember the goal— transformed lives.

Jesus had a small group of twelve men. We do not have word-for-word transcripts of everything they said and did during their three years together. Only the conversations that God decided we needed are given in the Gospels. No question they talked, laughed, had bad lunches together, and dealt with the elements. Together they dealt with grief, sickness, and hunger. So what was so transformational about this three-year relationship between Jesus and the disciples? You just read the answer! All of life, from the stormy seas to hunger pangs, was experienced with Jesus and one another. They were not just doing life. They were not just doing life together. But they were doing life together with Jesus.

The Five Myths about Smaller Communities

Small groups take a lot of work, and they can be difficult to implement effectively. They often struggle to be successful and transformational because of wrong expectations, beliefs, or myths about how they work best.

Myth 1: Your current small-group configuration is permanent. Jesus' small-group configuration was for about three years. Proof texting you might say? We don't think so. How important was this small group to God's plan? Our current small groups are direct descendents from that first one! The one method of a group represented by Jesus and the apostles would not be constituted as the killer app. But the group was a critical component. More was coming.

Notice also, much was going on in the discussions. All the discussions of the disciples did not happen while the facilitator (Jesus) was in the room.

The configuration and context changed after the Lord's ascension. New clusters developed. New people were introduced into the groups. A transformational group is one that adjusts as needed to encourage growth of the group and growth in the members of the group. Just as you rearrange the furniture in the house to accommodate changes in life, a group adjusts to accommodate changes in the community or church.

Being flexible with small-group meeting times and topics makes them fit Platte, South Dakota. The small-group structure of Calvary Baptist Church is fluid and diverse. According to Pastor Richard Slattery, the influence is from being part of a farming community. Work schedules vary dramatically. Small groups meet weekly, biweekly, mornings, midday, and night any day of the week. Men's, women's, mothers, and youth groups are among the diverse groups operating through Calvary. Pastor Richards also categorized several groups as being community wide and not particularly tied to the church. One group specifically mentioned had around fourteen who attend with only four people being connected to Calvary.

The community structure of a TC is dynamic. The structure in most churches is stagnant. In TCs, 69 percent of their members gave strong or moderate agreement to the idea that their church regularly starts new groups. For community to be transformative, new people must constantly be welcomed into the fellowship.

Myth 2: Small-group meeting locations are limited to church facilities or member homes. If small groups are transformational, the math is simple: More Groups = More Life Change.[2]

So here are a couple of key questions: What are some other places for small groups? How can you help facilitate them? How can you celebrate them? Small groups can gather at work, school, coffee shops, health clubs, or under a tree somewhere.

A practical question is, Where are small groups already naturally meeting? Service and leadership teams are one example. They gather in or around your church facility to take care of church responsibilities. Pastor John Terpstra of Immanuel Christian Reformed Church in Fort Collins, Colorado, believes community happens most effectively when church leaders gather for their ministry or planning. When discussing teams like deacons, missions, or fellowship teams, he said, "A lot of those people find small-group dynamics going on in their serving group. . . . They don't need another small group." According to Pastor Terpstra the group dynamics of a ministry team can fulfill the purpose of a small group.

With unlimited possibilities for the time and place of small-group community, TCs leverage every meeting for life change!

Myth 3: Your facilitator must be a highly trained spiritual superstar. Having a group of excellent teachers is good. But more than any other trait, small-group facilitators and Sunday School leaders need love for the people if you want to have transformational small groups. They need communication, resources, and encouragement. But they must, above all else, love God and His work in people.

If you place the standard for teaching skills too high, it can be counterproductive to your small-group structure. It can limit *how many groups you can multiply*. The goal of "excellent teaching" should be replaced with "effective teaching." Excellent teaching is characterized through teacher led and dominated class experience. Effective teaching is based upon taking class participants from where they are presently to a preferred future.

If your bar is too high, it will *discourage the development of future leaders*. If every teacher is basically a trained theologian, then the message sent to future group leaders is "nontheologians need not apply." Potential group leaders will feel unqualified and be hesitant to step into a leadership role. If we are seeking transformation, we must look for the potential that is in a leader where passion for transformation is apparent and skill can be developed along the way.

If information and doctrine are the main purposes of your groups, then recruit a schooled theologian. If life transformation is the goal, recruit those who show a clear and current pattern of transformation in their lives and who love to know and apply theological truths. The markers of a great small-group leader are simple and found in Luke 10:27, "'Love the Lord your God with all your heart, with all your soul, with all your strength and with all your mind'; and, 'your neighbor as yourself.'" If a small-group leader walks closely with God, then that leader will focus on the proper goals for the group.

Setting the standard for teaching skills too high will cause members to *choose groups based on the leader*. The dark side of recruiting only superstar leaders is reinforcing a celebrity-obsession mentality in the church. Our small communities ought to be consumed with seeing all lives changed, not personal entertainment by an astounding lesson week after week. When people choose attending a particular group solely because of the leader, it builds unhealthy competition between the groups and suppresses the missional impulse for multiplication. After all, who wants to go start over in a new group when Superman Stan is our teacher?

> *If life transformation is the goal, recruit those who show a clear and current pattern of transformation in their lives and who love to know and apply theological truths.*

We are not advocating throwing out all standards for small-group leaders. But we are asking you to think about where to set the bar that communicates the reason for pursuing community in the body of Christ.

Myth 4: Small-group organization must be complex. Simple is the word of the day. In fact, I (Thom) have written two books on the subject, *Simple Church* and *Simple Life*. If we want more groups and even a transforming movement of small groups throughout our community, then we will make things simple. Many of the reasons for simple have already been given in this current list of myths. The small-group system must not become so rigid that it is unchangeable.

We've both served effective churches with small groups and traditional Sunday School as our small-community delivery system. The complexity (which can be avoided) comes when the same leaders, in the same rooms, with mostly the same participants, spend extended time together. The lack of focus on a simple system that is easily reproducible results in a self-centered system that becomes inflexible over time.

Church leaders have two options at that point. Leave the inflexible groups alone and meet their perceived needs or challenge them to be a part of the vision for transformational small groups. Years ago, all age groups in the local church Sunday School participated in an annual "promotion" or a reshuffling of classes. The perception was that promotion was for children, which made perfect sense. When a kindergarten student moved to first grade, his class in church needed to change. But promotion and flexibility is for adults, too. Simple, fast, and flexible needs to be the design of your small group's delivery system no matter if it is small groups in the home or Sunday School. Life transformation is more likely in a simple and flexible environment.

Myth 5: Only pastors are qualified to administer pastoral care. As a church begins to grow, the paid staff is unable to keep pace with pastoral care needs. But people still need to be touched with grace, mercy, and sometimes admonished in their Christian walk. Unfortunately, many churches have adopted a clergification model of ministry. They consider missionaries the supremely spiritual people who go to far-flung places to preach. Pastors and staff are next, and they are paid to do the local ministry. Then there's the rest of us who "pay, pray, and get out of the way." The only problem—this is not a biblical system.

In TCs, we discovered that their volunteer leaders do pastoral care to the membership of the church.

- "When people are plugged into a small group at our church, they are ministered to and well cared for." (72 percent strongly or moderately agree)

Churches practicing transformational community expect that ministry can occur even when a person with "Reverend" before their name is not present. God knew we would all need a form of pastoral care, and so He formed the body of Christ with the necessary gifts and abilities to share His grace from one person to another. No professional degree required. Transformational small groups are alive with ministry to one another.

The Five Deliverables of Smaller Communities

Many churches choose off-campus small groups because they believe in the model as contextual for a new era or they cannot afford to build enough church facilities. Others do Sunday School because they believe it is most effective. This is a good time to repeat, a group is a group. Call it whatever you like, meet whenever and wherever you want. So what can a transformational small community add to your church? What does the group deliver for the mission of God and the cause of Christ?

What does it look life when someone's life is being transformed by a small-group connection? Gwen described her small-group experience to her pastor this way:

> So . . . I'm here—they're here—God's here. I don't know them— they don't know me. But . . . God knows us all so we do have something in common.
>
> We have our study materials—we have our Bibles. We begin to study His Word, we pray together, and we ask God's Spirit to speak to us individually and corporately. Slowly, at first, I begin to share my questions, my struggles, my praises, and my experiences. Our relationship with one another begins.
>
> I don't know when it happened exactly, but these once strangers, have become an important part of my daily life. I don't wait for our weekly meetings anymore to get caught up with everyone. We call, e-mail, Facebook, chat, text, and see each other throughout the week. We serve together, we serve each other, we listen, we encourage each other, and yes, we have fun together! God's presence is undeniable and that is what all the excitement is about![3]

What if Gwen's experience was part of every Christian's journey in your local church? The results of a personal connection to a smaller group of Christians would be astounding. This is not to suggest small groups are perfect or easy. Here is the dirty little secret for those who believe small groups in homes are "the more excellent way." Small groups can be a real pain. Wherever they happen, for groups to work well, work must happen, too. We have yet to discover "five ways to make groups easy." When we do, that will be a book, we guarantee.

I (Ed) believe in small community not because I always enjoy it. I have been in small groups where I have been confronted. I have been in small groups that had conflict. I have been in small groups that had the life drained out of them because of issues. It is easier to sit face forward in the stands watching the show on the field (an entertainment model of public worship gatherings). But that is an easy religion not found in the New Testament church. It is easy to watch the show, but it is biblical to gather in small communities and to live on mission. God made us for community. A small community owning a great mission for the glory of God and the redemption of the peoples of the world is worth it.

So what is the *why* of smaller communities? Let's look at how the activity of community results in transformed lives.

Deliverable 1: Smaller communities deliver deeper friendships. Cheers was a highly successful television comedy in the 1980s and 1990s about a bar and its patrons in Boston, Massachusetts. A mailman, a psychiatrist, an accountant, and others met daily around the bar to drink and talk about life. The theme song of the show described the small group as a place where, "Everybody knows your name." We all have that need: to belong to a group where everybody knows your name.

As our churches continue to grow larger, they must also grow smaller to connect people on a transformational level. We may not like to admit it, but we know when we are known, and we like it better that way. It has been said that our own name is the sweetest word in the world to us. Nothing is more personal and unique. Nothing gets a quicker or more emotional response.

For transformation to take place, we must know and invest in relationships with one

> *A small community owning a great mission for the glory of God and the redemption of the people of the world is worth it.*

another. By joining other Christians in small-group communities, believers can find the environment where life change can often occur most readily.

Deliverable 2: Smaller communities deliver accountability relationships. Big groups provide inspiration and information. But they also provide an overabundance of anonymity. The anonymity comes in handy when you don't want to show up or sign up. Church leaders can appeal from the large-group platform until they are blue in the face. They can invest hours and hours producing video clips if they want. The large group provides cover for not giving, not serving, not praying, or not inviting others. We are just another face in the crowd. Who will know? Accountability is absent in the large gathering.

The most valuable takeaway in a smaller community is the person sitting beside me. Our lives become a weekly narrative to one another of God's faithfulness and our response. Connecting to a small group of friends means that we leave our halo at the door. The accountability living in a class or group helps us to live in the transformation brought about by the Christ.

If we desire to be missional, then our lives must honor the One who sent us. In a church I was serving, a couple came to me (Ed) and reported, "Pastor, we have decided to get divorced." I said, "No!" They replied, "We were not coming for permission." I explained to them that we had chosen to live together in biblical community. We can't let this happen. Our lives are more shaped by the gospel because we hold one another accountable for the gospel. We become a sign of the kingdom of God. Accountable relationships promote the church looking more like the kingdom of God; therefore it can live on mission.

It might sound a bit strange, but the local church needs more provoking. We read, "And let us be concerned about one another in order to promote love and good works, not staying away from our meetings, as some habitually do, but encouraging each other, and all the more as you see the day drawing near" (Heb. 10:24–25). In the KJV the word *promote* is translated "provoke," which provides a more vivid picture. We like the word *provoke* because it feels a bit more aggressive . . . of course in a positive,

Christian way. Our nature is to be a sinner and drift away from God and His purposes. We need a bit of positive provocation to keep us on path through the accountability of friends.

So small groups cannot be just another program provided to those interested in . . . small groups. Smaller communities must be part of a commitment to spur one another on in our Christian commitment.

Deliverable 3: Smaller communities deliver environments for spiritual growth. Attraction may get someone in the front door of a church on Sunday morning. The unchurched, previously churched, and church shoppers are looking for excitement, energy, and creativity. Churches have never been better at producing solid Sunday morning environments. But relational connection and life transformation in small groups will move them beyond the spectator level.

Also, what attracts them into the front door will not translate into personal transformation even if they attend multiple times. Initially they may only feel comfortable enjoying and engaging at a distance, but something must make them more involved in the action. One visit a week or a few visits a month are less evasive with less results. The nature of a smaller group results in another connecting point. In most churches new attendees only see multiple layers of structure and little relational space. Connecting them to a small community is critical for their spiritual journey.

Transformational Churches know how to simplify vision and concepts in ways people can absorb quickly. Churches may use different words as descriptors, but you will often see Transformational Churches finding ways to remind people what is the ultimate "deliverable." A simple visual may communicate all of this in a way that helps people grasp each small-group deliverable with one word.

Deliverable 1: Connect

Deliverable 2: Grow

Deliverable 3: Serve

Deliverable 4: Go

(Note: Go to www.lifeway.com/adultstrategy to learn more about the CGSG Strategy.)

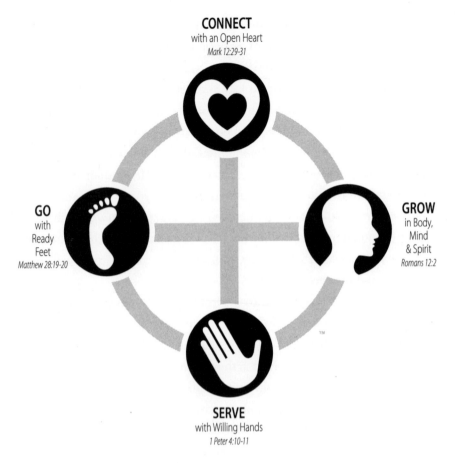

CONNECT
with an Open Heart
Mark 12:29-31

GO
with
Ready
Feet
Matthew 28:19-20

GROW
in Body,
Mind
& Spirit
Romans 12:2

SERVE
with Willing Hands
1 Peter 4:10-11

Many church sanctuaries are designed the same way. We find seats on an ascending upward floor so that everyone feels close to the action. It's been the normal way to design churches. But it has an unintentional side effect. It implies that the action is on the platform, and the people in the seats are there to cheer and enjoy the game. The attendees are the fans and cheerleaders, the players are the preachers and musicians.

In Transformational Churches there are no stands but all fields. The small groups in a TC serve to help people change, grow, and become more like Jesus. A smaller community puts me in the locker room and out on the field wearing the team jersey. Action does take energy and add to the "busy" in our lives. But action is what God uses to go deeper in the lives of people and to keep them engaged in His adventure.

Deliverable 4: Smaller communities deliver maximum participation. Even the normal size church (seventy-five on Sunday morning) is driven by its worship service and is limited in the number of people who can participate. Transformational small groups require more than just attendance. Attendees must take responsibility for the long-term functionality of the group. The more responsibilities can be distributed, the healthier the group becomes. We believe in small communities that give everyone a job. Prayer leaders, home hosts, greeters, communications leaders, facilitators, and community mission leaders are just a few job opportunities in a small group. Normally small-group jobs are simple and do not require knowledge or experience. The group belongs to the group. When we get maximum participation, we get maximum buy-in for people engaged in God's mission. That matters.

> *Transformational Churches know how to simplify vision and concepts in ways people can absorb quickly.*

People need to move from sitting in rows to sitting in circles. Sitting in rows you are watching someone else using their gifts. You are more a passive spectator than an active participant. Small groups help people move from sitting in rows to sitting in circles and from sitting in circles to going into the world.

Deliverable 5: Smaller communities deliver missional opportunities. The small groups in your church must be more than social or study groups. If they are biblical communities, something else must happen. They must be filled with people who hold to a missionary mentality ready to engage in the mission of the church. Mission will provide the glue for the group.

As we wrote earlier, the group and classes will serve to minister to the members. But to keep the members ever transforming to look like Jesus, they must be given the opportunity to help the community reflect the kingdom of God. The goal of a group must be the multiplication of disciples for Jesus.

The Five Obstacles Facing Transformational Small Communities

Unfortunately, small-group ministries face challenges and obstacles that hinder transformation in and through small communities.

The first obstacle to transformational small communities is that the transference of information is valued much more than life transformation. Biblical illiteracy is a problem in North America and even the church. But the work of a small group or Sunday School class does not end when the members can all find Thessalonica on the map in the back of their Bibles. The purpose of community must be to engender the desire and see the effects of transformation. Somewhere between biblical literacy and biblical minutia we find spiritual maturity. Knowledge puffs up and cannot be the goal alone. Transformation includes biblical learning, but it does not end with it.

> **People need to move from sitting in rows to sitting in circles.**

Another obstacle to transformational small communities is that teaching is valued more than learning. We have already pointed out the danger of only recruiting the uber-qualified as leaders for classes and groups. The goal must be that people are joyfully learning, not that one person is happy teaching. Leaders should focus as much on application of the truth as the delivery of it. For small groups to be transformational, they should include monologue and dialogue. Leaders of groups should always have these questions in mind:

- How well are members applying God's truth?
- Where is each participant with the Lord?

Remember the agenda is Christ being formed in the lives of those involved in your small group.

The third obstacle to small communities is when they become a reflection of past practices. Churches with a strong history and tradition of Sunday School can be closed to deeper discussions and questions. They have done groups a certain way for years. The way is safe. The connection is important.

Ironically, my experience (Ed) has shown that newer churches do not take long to become inflexible in group life. They just set up a smaller pulpit, stifling meaningful interaction. Group life is a tool of God for His purposes, not an institutional expectation. Groups provide the opportunity to live life on life.

The fourth small communities obstacle is a segmentation of the mission of God. The mission of small communities is not to teach the Bible only. Every expression of church owns all the mission of God. Your smaller community owns the mission of God. You have been called and empowered. The danger of segmentation is great. The smaller communities say that is not their role. *Our purpose is to get through the study,* they think. Every small group needs to adopt a nation in the world. We are going to go. We are going to connect. We own the mission of God.

Located on a dirt road in Mississippi is a tiny Pentecostal church. The building is about the size of a two-car garage. I (Ed) was traveling in Mississippi when I passed the Pentecostal World Outreach Center. The church would seat twenty-five people at the most. Yet the church sign announcing their identity to people in the community was as large as the church. The sign stretched ten feet across and eight feet tall. I was so inspired I wanted a picture. They were right—they, and every church, is a world outreach center.

God's mission belongs to every believer everywhere. TCs understand that the mission of God must be inherent in the DNA of every small group. Sunday School classes must see making disciples as their responsibility and privilege. Small groups in homes must adopt transforming lives and communities as their primary work. We all own this one mission, and the small-group ministry of a church can be its launching point, production system, and fulfillment deliverer.

The fifth small communities obstacle is a lack of intimacy. We use the term community freely, yet there are multiple layers of community. Community in a broad sense is achieved around common interests. The most concrete example of community is your local neighborhood. You may not have any significant conversations with your neighbors, even though you have lived

> **God's mission belongs to every believer everywhere.**

on the same street for years. Normally if there is a series of break-ins on your block or another neighborhood crisis, you start talking to your neighbors. You now share a common interest: the security of your personal property. Although new friendships can begin because of the mutual interest and corresponding conversations, you only experience community on a shallow level.

The next level of community is critical for a smaller group to become transformational. The word is *communitas*. *Communitas* is a threshold or space where deeper sharing and conversations take place. The dynamic of a deeper level or threshold of sharing is not automatic. The smaller group becomes a safe zone where deeper questions and struggles can be discussed. The environment is relaxed and open. People can pray for one another in the moment. People can pray (and do in a transformational small group) beyond living rooms and meeting times. More conversations evolve outside the meeting. Actions and accountability take place. Christ is formed in members because of the environment God creates in the group, not just because there was a meeting.[4]

The Five Elements of a Transformational Small-Group Environment

Small-group ministry is by nature organic. All relationships that last normally occur because people feel naturally drawn together. However, we have observed that TCs are intentional about building community through specific elements. We've seen that the following five such elements are regularly seen in transformational small groups.

1. Mission orientation: Focus must go toward joining God on His mission. Every group needs a mission beyond their group. Remember, every born-again believer is responsible for the world. Growth and maturity happen just as much on mission as on knowledge. How much more can you learn on mission? How can you say you are growing and maturing in your faith without mission?

2. *Word-driven mentality:* Sharing is important for the group to go deeper. However, the anchor of a transformational small group is the Word of God. When a group establishes *communitas*, that is a good thing, yet new challenges emerge. Sharing can become an end to itself and can become the entire agenda. Sharing more deeply in any context can become cathartic and, thus, of great value. But the context of sharing must be established so that a small group does not become an emotional support group. The emotionally needy can dominate sharing times. Also the environment for the new people can be uncomfortable when a deep level of sharing is their first group experience. We think you see the dilemma.

A group needs to be welcoming and a group needs to establish *communitas*. Those two elements can appear contradictory. One way to overcome the contradiction is to establish a Word-driven mentality. It begins, returns, and ends with God's Word. God's Word becomes relevant to any challenge or discussion. A great reframing question for the group is, What does God say that might address this issue? And these great questions: Is there an example in Scripture of someone who faced a similar issue? How did they respond? How did that work for them?

As Jesus' disciples processed life with Him, we see a continual conversation. The disciples were needy. Their needs were constantly the topic of conversation. Yet Jesus did not let the needs of the group dominate. Instead He taught them His truth in order to keep them oriented on the kingdom that brings transformation rather than human opinion which derails change.

3. *Multiplication mindset:* Groups must understand from day one that their purpose is to reproduce. Apprentices to the group leader should share responsibilities with the leader and prepare to launch the next group. Not only does this help groups remain fluid and flexible, but it helps group life become more accessible to new people.

Multiplication is often stifled in churches due to a caste system of ministry. Over time the church has developed the three-tiered system we described earlier that defines who can do what in the church. The lowest tier is the laity. The assumed position for them is to do the grunt work, participate in the programs, and follow the leaders' orders. Second is the tier of professional ministers. The pastors and paid church staff hold specialized training and are given the positions of leadership for the church. The final tier is that of missionary. It is reserved for the "super spiritual" who are held in an almost patron-saint manner.

TCs have chosen to place ministry and leadership into the lives of believers. They understand that the New Testament pattern is for Christians to find their place in the body of Christ and serve the mission of the kingdom. From the statements in the TC survey, notice the high level of agreement in the TCs.

- "We diminish the distinction between 'clergy' and 'laity' and encourage everyone to minister." (68 percent strongly or moderately agree)
- "Church members are expected to serve in a ministry at our church." (58 percent strongly or moderately agree)
- "We celebrate and highlight volunteers who serve." (55 percent strongly or moderately agree)
- "Our church helps people understand their spiritual gifts." (58 percent strongly or moderately agree)
- "Serving is considered normal behavior at our church." (71 percent strongly or moderately agree)

Multiplication can happen in the church through the leadership of a few members of the professional clergy. But that multiplication is dwarfed in comparison to a TC that has unleashed its members to lead and serve in the ministry of transforming a community.

Pastor John Terpstra and Immanuel Christian Reformed Church in Fort Collins, Colorado, empowers laity to lead groups through an organic approach. Pastor Terpstra described their approach:

"Our small-group ministry would be a group of people not staff driven, not leader driven by any official person in the church.

Generally they're between five and ten people who make a commitment to meet in each other's homes on a rotating basis on an average of every other week or once a month."

He considers a healthy small-group process one that is operating organically.

"It's been interesting, though, over this last year. Once we got some momentum around that, people are forming groups and adding members to their groups, and they're not telling me. I take that as success. When someone comes up to me, and I say, 'Have you ever thought about being in a small group?' and the answer is, 'Yes, I was invited to one six months ago, and I joined, was that OK?' And I go, 'Yes, that was absolutely fine.' So it's kind of self-managed now that we've created a cluster of small groups."

4. Stranger welcoming: Groups must always be concerned about the empty chair. Intentionality is critical here. Groups do not welcome new people as well as they think they do. A welcoming environment goes beyond a warm greeting and directions to the food table. As groups become focused on themselves, they leave little relational space for the comfortable entry of new people.

5. Kingdom focused: What does it mean for a transformational small group to be kingdom focused? Groups are work. We have established

> *Multiplication is dwarfed in comparison to a TC that has unleashed its members to lead and serve in the ministry of transforming a community.*

that fact. Groups will naturally drift toward some unhealthy waters if left on their own. First, they will become church obsessed. The first drift is a result of small thinking and limits what God really wants from your group. Groups can be approached by well-meaning members as that thing we do that makes their church better than the others. Groups can validate us, in our minds, as innovative, bold, and fun. Members tell their friends, "Our church is so great because we have groups. Come to our group so you can see how great our church is." The second default is even smaller. Our group is about me. The group is about me because my life is a wreck and I need group help. I need people in the group to bring me meals, to help me fix my car, and to hear me cry to console me. Groups are about the greater kingdom of God. They must find their purpose beyond emotional support to be a significant part of God's plan for transformation.

Conclusion

Templo Rosa De Saron Spanish Assembly of God in Salinas, California, is committed to reaching hurting people in their community through their small groups. Salinas is a region of 150,000 people with 65 percent being Hispanic. Known as the "the Salad Bowl of the World," Salinas, and the Salinas Valley, is an agricultural community worldwide producer of broccoli, lettuce, and mushrooms.

Pastor Manuel Dorado has extensive experience in a process of raising leaders and multiplying groups to reach communities. Pastor Dorado had been involved in a cell-based church. As a youth minister at a Filipino church in suburban Los Angeles he learned from the Korean cell model.

Pastor Dorado developed his approach based on the "G12 Model"[5] originating in Bogotá, Columbia. Fundamentally, he starts with twelve people, trains them, and they start groups. One of the keys to the success of small groups at Templo Rosa is the pastor leading the group leaders as a small group. To make the whole church a small-group church, the pastor must have group leaders as his small group. As they do life together, they focus on their personal spiritual growth as well as their development as leaders. Finding and training leaders is the core of their success. "You can only grow as fast as you can find and train leaders," according to Pastor Dorado.

> *Groups are about the greater kingdom of God. They must find their purpose beyond emotional support to be a significant part of God's plan for transformation.*

New group leaders find participants among their peers, friends, and neighbors. Then they work on leading them to become a Christian.

Life change—transformation—is the target. They hope for "healing of the sick and sick at heart." They also seek to save marriages and reconcile relationships (especially fathers and sons in the Hispanic community).

Pastor Dorado calls their groups "home groups" as opposed to Bible study because the purpose of the groups is evangelism. Groups often start through neighborhood events. Included in group life are fellowship, Bible study, once-a-month celebrations, and meeting needs. Most members of the cell groups do not attend Templo Rosa De Saron initially. Groups value being warm and welcoming. Over time, as friends and neighbors get acquainted with the groups, they often attend the church. Small groups function as a front door to the Christian faith and church life.

> One clear principle emerges—biblical Christianity cannot be lived out through larger-group experiences alone.

By looking at smaller groups in Transformational Churches, important patterns emerge. Groups are diverse and predominately lay driven. Some are study driven; others are more relational. In every context and model are examples of significant life change and fulfillment of the mission of God. One clear principle emerges—biblical Christianity cannot be lived out through larger-group experiences alone. The monologue must change to dialogue and the conversation must be ongoing. The journey with Jesus cannot be lived in anonymity.

In the end, transformation happens in the context of a relationship with God. He does not need the church or other Christians to be involved. But He has chosen for us to be involved. God chose to use vocabulary such as the body, household, and family to describe the church. He wants us to be in relationship with one another. The work we see the church do in its earliest days informs our present. The church works in community with one another just as the Father, Son, and Spirit work in relationship to one another.

Members in Transformational Churches thus engage God in worship. They engage each other in community. But they also engage the world in mission. That is the subject of our next chapter.

9
Mission: Show Jesus through Word and Action

As the Father has sent me, so send I you.

(John 20:21)

Story of Success

I (Ed) am writing this as I fly back from the Verge Conference sponsored by Austin Stone Community Church, Austin, Texas. The church is engaged in its community and living out its faith in many ways. Pastor Matt Carter explained:

> At the Austin Stone, we are attempting to be a church for the city. Many churches are simply in a city. Some churches are actually against their city, but we are attempting to be for it. In other words, we aren't just seeking the spiritual flourishing of Austin

but its economic, educational and cultural flourishing as well. We believe that as our love of the city grows, our influence in it will grow, making inroads for our ability to preach and deliver the gospel in the city.

One of our main structures in which we are implementing this strategy is "missional communities." In short, it is a small-group structure in which the groups live out the gospel in the sphere of influence God has placed them. Instead of a small-group environment built around Bible study and dips and chips, it is a group of people living incarnationally in an attempt to be salt and light to their neighborhoods, boardrooms and classrooms of the city of Austin.

TRANSFORMATIONAL LEADERS SPEAK . . .

"Good news and accompanying good deeds are like the two wings of an airplane. Each is incomplete without the other. Each complements the other. Each gives 'lift' to the other. To study the life and ministry of Jesus is to study a tapestry woven of good news and good deeds."[1] —Eric Swanson, *The Externally Focused Church*

Creating Safe Places for Gospel Conversations

Bridges help people cross over divides. We believe there are bridges churches can use across which the gospel can travel. Missionaries have talked of such for years—finding connections with culture to help people connect with one another so they can be in natural conversations—in the same place and personal space. And, bridges are different from one culture to another—they depend on the context.

Crossville United Methodist Church joins with the Christian Hunters Association for an outreach event called Bubbafest. Crossville is a town of around twelve thousand located between Knoxville and Nashville, Tennessee. Bubbafest is held prior to the opening of deer season. Their gym and stage morph into the "largest deer head display in the country." Hunters have come from as far away as Iowa. As many as three thousand people have attended the event over the past two years. Local churches partner together and provide free food. The sanctuary is turned into a duck blind. The church is filled with hunting displays. Displays are open to both churched and unchurched people. Pastor John Halliberton said, "We brought in people who put on camouflage and normally never come to church."

> **Bridges help people cross over divides.**

The success of the event is not measured by innovation or popularity alone. Clear presentations of the gospel and challenges to respond to Christ's invitation to faith are part of the event. Various speakers present the gospel to the group through personal testimonies of how they embraced faith in Christ. Transformational Churches create environments to present the gospel of Jesus Christ. They train, model, and create platforms to invite people to cross the line of faith and follow Jesus Christ.

Engaging the Mission

Transformational Churches have found a way for the convergence of value and activities to result in something specific—transformed lives. Without this key element the rest of the work does not mean much. The reason for the church's existence is to increase the fame of God through the redemption of people. With that in mind, we turn our attention to how TCs fulfill the mission of the church, namely making disciples who join Jesus on mission.

Transformational Churches engage people in ministry within the church and mission outside the church. One of the first lessons learned about a church with transformational practices is that evangelism is a natural part of life for its members. Because it stands as the heart of the church, sharing their faith in Christ is natural for the members. The church has made a conscious decision that their existence is directly related to God's mission of seeing people reconciled through Christ. Some had evangelism training and mass evangelistic events. Many did not. But all had an evangelistic passion.

Churches in our study were less engaged in formal evangelism training although they were distinctly evangelistic. Yet we believe formal evangelism training has value. In fact, training people in the aspects of the gospel and defending our faith is necessary in our day of decrease in the number of believers in North America. However, the studies told by TCs indicate that they rely less on "canned evangelism" and more on naturally occurring evangelistic encounters.

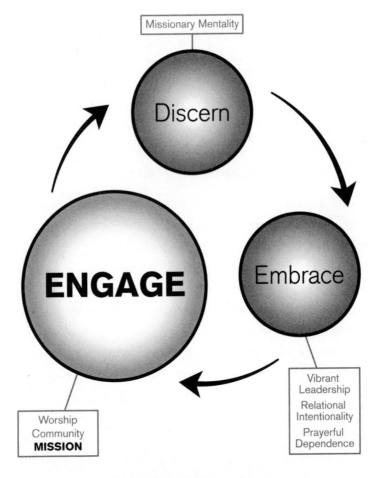

Transformational Loop

- "Our church challenges members to build significant relationships with people who are non-Christian." (30 percent strongly agree)

Relational evangelism has been a popular phrase for some time. However, it is difficult to define. More often we must describe what relational evangelism looks like rather than define it. In TCs we have seen a general environment that encourages faith sharing in everyday life rather than at specific times (events, home visits) on the church calendar. In the above statistic, notice how high the percentage even just looking at the "strongly agreed" category. Again, though we think evangelism training is important, TCs seem to have a greater number of people who share their faith out of the overflow of the rest of their Christian experience.

> TCs seem to have a greater number of people who share their faith out of the overflow of the rest of their Christian experience.

Another facet of disciple making we discovered in TCs was the relationship between evangelism and community ministry. Churches with transformational practices were active—even aggressive—about service in the community. But TCs place an emphasis on social ministry only as far as it serves the purpose of sharing the gospel. The engagement in compassion ministries did not serve as an end to itself but a way to communicate the reason for the service—namely the message of redemption in Christ.

Transformational Churches have a significantly higher percentage of believers who see their church engaged in a deeper mission.

- "Our church intentionally provides service opportunities for our people to be engaged with the unchurched in our local city or community." (33 percent strongly agree)

Although they want their local church to grow in attendance they understand that the mission is much greater. Again, this is seen in the above response by just reporting the "strongly agree" category. Rather than merely inviting their city to the church they are committed to take their church to the city. The drive to serve comes from a passion for God and a vital relationship with Him. Significance and the approval of others are not important to these members who are taught to be missionaries to their culture. The mission is about God and His desire for the community. The level of maturity is greater than complying in the flesh. The power of God in the life of a missionary believer involves thinking of yourself less, not thinking less of yourself.

- "Our church celebrates when members serve the local city or community." (53 percent strongly or moderately agree)
- "People regularly become Christians as a result of our church serving." (44 percent strongly or moderately agree)

> *Transformational Churches have a significantly higher percentage of believers who see their church engaged in a deeper mission.*

TCs have a different perspective on church membership. It is not just signing a card at the front of the church. They spread the vision that members are local missionaries. Membership is equated with a commitment to both the church and to serve the gospel to the community.

When considering the incredible shift in the spiritual life of North America, some feel afraid. The trends are disturbing. People are without Christ. Churches are closing. Are we seeing the beginning of the end of Christianity in North America? Are we destined to become another story like our friends in Europe? Like attempting to turn the *Titanic*, mere concern will not get the job done.

The North American Religious Identification Survey is research based on responses to one key question, What is your religion, if any? Surveyors were instructed to record the exact answer given to that question. The question was open-ended, so there were no multiple-choice options. So you have a true, self-identification survey. The answers were not verified with local or national churches. And, as with any survey, the "halo effect" is always considered. People tend to answer questions in a way that makes them look or feel better. The survey was taken with a statistically significant sample in 1990, 2001, and 2008. More than 200,000 people were contacted by both home and cell phones during those three years. Although any research has shortcomings, at least we are able to compare the results in the three surveys to identify religious trends. What can we learn from the research?

- Fewer North Americans are identifying themselves as "Christian."
- One in five adults did not identify with any religion (doubled since 1990).
- "Nones" or those who claimed no religious affiliation grew 138 percent since 1990.[2]

The results of ARIS show us that the modern world is not so different from the ancient cultures of the Roman Empire and beyond. The apostle Paul presented the message of Jesus to a world that had never known Him. We do the same. Perhaps the numbers were more challenging than we ever faced in North America, but God used Paul in unimaginable ways as a missionary witness.

For example, being a missionary in Thessalonica in AD 52 was no easy task. Both Jew and Gentile hated Christians equally. Eventually, Paul and Silas were forced to leave. They traveled to Berea where they found a different level of receptivity to the gospel. "The people here [Berea] were more open-minded than those in Thessalonica, since they welcomed the message with eagerness and examined the Scriptures daily to see if these things were so" (Acts 17:11). The approach by the early missionaries was simple. When approaching a hostile or disinterested culture with the gospel, patience and immersion in the culture were keys. Paul and others chose to live and work among the people. Although impossible to know the specifics, evidence suggests Paul's mission team planted themselves for an extended period of time, even in places not initially receptive to the gospel.

We learn that to live as a missionary is to live and work among the people. "For you remember our labor and hardship, brothers. Working night and day so that we would not burden any of you, we preached God's gospel to you. You are witnesses, and so is God, of how devoutly, righteously, and blamelessly we conducted ourselves with you believers" (1 Thess. 2:9–10). The description of doing life alongside a deeply loved people, modeling Christ, and explaining the truth about God to those who would listen was being a missionary in Thessalonica. Early believers desired transformation of the lost more than they desired comfort for themselves. The emphasis on seeing people changed by the power of Christ must outweigh other desires. In TCs today, the same emphasis persists.

For years Christians in North America had the luxury of depending on attractive churches and programs to be their proxy evangelist to our culture. It is "bricks and mortar" evangelism. The church facility and the corresponding activity served as the entity tasked to draw the lost to Jesus. In past years, in specific regions in the U.S., this approach to evangelism worked. But the track record of success in the past is not always good.

An entire segment of our current Christian population believes that giving, building, and inviting is good enough to keep the church on track as the evangelist to our culture. Some Christians think that if lost people could only hear the pastor preach then God will take care of the rest. As our culture becomes increasingly less churched (or interested in church), we are forced to move our methods further back in history to a more ancient approach to reaching people. Some call this the transition from the *come and see* evangelist church to a post-Christendom *go and tell* missionary church. That is not to say that "come and see" is over. It's not. But we need more "go and tell."

The church is no longer (in most places) the local evangelist. It is now the missionary. Being buried in the culture to display Christ in daily life is a critical issue. If the church is positioned in culture as the missionary, the members must learn to live like it. Terms like *making disciples, outreach,* and *evangelism* must be understood in the larger framework of the mission of God. God glorifies Himself through the transformation of sinners into saints. God's mission is entrusted to us to be missionaries in a world to

which we hold no allegiance. Rather, we are
ambassadors on a mission to persuade all others
to follow the King.

> *It is not to say
> that "come and
> see" is over.
> It's not. But we
> need more "go
> and tell."*

By watching Paul, we see that intentionality
is a key element to being effective on our mission
for God. Being a missionary does not happen
naturally. A quick flyover of Paul and Silas making tents for a living reveals much. The church
was brand new. People did not get the tithing thing yet. New churches
were populated with mere babes in Christ. The staff needed to get a job to
help support themselves, right? But Paul and Silas were not working just
to raise financial support for their mission. Working was a major part of
their mission. Paul and Silas were not waiting for opportunities to show
and tell the gospel. They were cultivating opportunities to make disciples
intentionally.

Engaging Fully in the Mission

The mission of the church is to glorify God and make disciples. But
that is easier to type and say than to do. As we have looked into the TCs
of our studies, their stories show that they are willing to invest deeper into
the mission than other churches. The focus of a church with transformational practices is on moving the mission forward, as opposed to coddling
immature believers. Engaging the lost, winning the lost, and maturing
believers to repeat the process was the pervasive mission in the TCs we
encountered.

So what does a real missionary church look like? The missionary activity of Paul and Silas provides the biblical picture for the Transformational
Church engaged in God's mission.

The first step to engaging in God's mission is to define success. The missionary report from Paul to Christians in Thessalonica was clear and confident. He reported, "For you yourselves know, brothers, that our visit with
you was not without result" (1 Thess. 2:1). Paul said the trip was not a waste

of time. How did Paul know there were results? He looked for the tangible and intangible measurements for the church.

Even when under the duress of being brought before King Agrippa, he spoke of his conversion and the need for all to trust Christ. "Therefore, King Agrippa, I was not disobedient to the heavenly vision. Instead, I preached to those in Damascus first, and to those in Jerusalem and in all the region of Judea, and to the Gentiles, that they should repent and turn to God, and do works worthy of repentance" (Acts 26:19–20). The DNA of his early days of belief was the foundation for a missionary life of obedience regardless of the response. The missionary calling defined Paul's identity.

Some churches have weak scorecards. We do good things, but we miss the great things because we do not have a predetermined picture of success. A willingness to serve, a good attitude, and high attendance goals are good but need to be placed in perspective. They are not wrong or senseless scorecards, but they should be secondary measurements. We must look to see the number being brought into relationship to Christ and then how they are being matured in their faith.

- "In our church, we believe that relationships with unchurched people are critical to the mission of advancing the gospel." (78 percent of TC members strongly or moderately agree)

The transformational activity we should crave is advancing the gospel into the lives of unbelievers. The gospel is not something you easily get over. It is something you will live in. A cross-centered and resurrection-powered life no longer lives for itself. Or it shouldn't. Instead, it dies daily for the new priority of the kingdom's mission.

We need to measure the mission and the transformation in people's lives. The way you measure success should be clearly understood by everyone in your church. From the senior staff to the ushers, to the nursery workers, everyone should be able to identify the business of the church. In TCs it happens regularly. The staff and people of a church know what is most important because they are taught it, hear it consistently from the leaders, and have decided to live out the mission instead of being enslaved by secondary traditions.

Paul was able to report with confidence because he knew the missionary scorecard. He wrote: "For the Lord's message rang out from you, not only in Macedonia and Achaia, but in every place that your faith in God has gone out, so we don't need to say anything. For they themselves report about us what kind of reception we had from you: how you turned to God from idols to serve the living and true God" (1 Thess. 1:8–9). Transformational mission work will cause people to drop their dead idol and embrace the living Christ.

Paul was driven with great passion and commitment to see life change. God is calling His church to measure success first by transformed lives. TCs know their mission and how to assess effectiveness at fulfilling their mission. Assessment is critical in order to know that lives are being transformed. How do I measure life change? Each church has to decide the answer, but a decision must be made. Is life change assessed through changes in attitude, behavior, or both? Is life change measured by evidence of engagement in spiritual disciplines or church involvement?

> The gospel is not something you easily get over. It is something you will live in.

The TC scorecard should have the heading: Lives being visibly transformed by the power of Christ. Everybody who serves or leads should know clearly what the heading is. They should talk and pray about it constantly. Changed lives are the obsession of a Transformational Church.

The second step to engaging God's mission is to prepare. When teaching a teenager to drive, only the most irresponsible parent would simply hand over the keys to the family car and say, "The interstate is in that direction. Good luck. Don't wreck it." Rather, parents show the teenager how to drive first. Then they make sure the soon-to-be driver is educated in the traffic laws. Then, when they put them behind the wheel for the first time, it is in a parking lot or other place where there is no other traffic. You see where we are going. The first time teenagers drive alone, they have been well prepared for the experience.

In the Transformational Church survey, we found the same to be true in the area of preparing believers for the mission of God. They were prepared. They received training to be on mission. But, as you will read, the preparation was often different from what we normally see in North American churches.

Preparation for evangelizing. The preparation by TCs is different from what we see occurring in other churches. When dealing with the mission of God, we normally think about weekly evangelism training meetings accompanied by visitation programs. In the TCs we surveyed, we did not find the elusive "magic bullet" that prepared the entire congregation in one method of mission.

The research discovered that churches with this transformational practice prepare their people for mission in a multitude of ways. Some offered evangelism training of some sort, though we did not see formal evangelism training as the norm. More often it came in the form of Bible study groups discussing doctrinal issues or cultural engagement and a church-wide passion for personal engagement. When training was present, it was to help people do what they were already passionate about.

The preparation for mission came often in the form of mentoring and coaching new leaders. Once again we see that the convergence of elements is what makes a TC. And for the mission to be at the forefront of its activities requires leadership and the fellowship's involvement for individual growth.

Preparation for opposition. Opposition is inevitable for a church or Christian that fully engages the mission of God. The North American church does not face the persecution we read about in the book of Acts or from missionary reports from believers in the Middle or Far East today. But we will face spiritual opposition at every turn from Satan.

The apostle Paul knew this and reported, "On the contrary, after we had previously suffered and been outrageously treated in Philippi, as you know, we were emboldened by our God to speak the gospel of God to you in spite of great opposition" (1 Thess. 2:2). The word for "opposition" in the passage is an athletic term that describes an opponent in a game or match. In any assignment from God, we must realize that the other side exists. The opposition is not merely intellectual or philosophical. It is spiritual in origin. The mission of Satan is to stop those who are on the mission of God.

Paul, earlier in his conversation with King Agrippa, unapologetically identified the source of resistance to his missionary calling. Paul told the king what God told him verbatim: "I will rescue you from the people and from the Gentiles, to whom I now send you, to open their eyes that they may turn from darkness to light and from the power of Satan to God, that they may receive forgiveness of sins and a share among those who are sanctified by faith in Me" (Acts 26:17–19). The lost, as innocent as they may look when you drive through your city, are people under the power of Satan. Satan wants to keep them there! As people are prepared to engage the mission of God, proper training and willpower is not enough for success. There is an opposing side.

TCs experience an ongoing convergence of elements when it comes to the mission of the church. Prayerful dependence, an emphasis on community between believers, and the mission make for a powerful defense as they converge on the field of ministry.

Training is valued. The stories from TCs showed that the members of these churches expected and valued the training they received to be active in the mission of the church. Many pastors have been in the unenviable circumstance of planning an evangelistic training course and only a handful of people show up. On further review they are the same people who show up to every training course. Every church has a few people who are committed to evangelism, mission in the community, and being trained. In TCs training is valued on a much wider scale. They expect that their lives as well as lives in the community will be transformed because of the missional environment.

We want to make a critical distinction. Perhaps it is a warning of sorts. Much of what passes as training is actually just orientation. Orientation just lets you know what is out there, what is upcoming. Training prepares you to handle the circumstances adeptly. Think about what happens each time a commercial airliner is preparing to close the door and prepare for takeoff. A flight attendant walks down the aisle to the people sitting in the exit rows. She or he asks the passengers if they are prepared to open the door in case of an emergency landing and perhaps gives a brief overview of what it takes to open the door. At best it is merely an orientation to where you are and what is required of you.

> *Prayerful dependence, an emphasis on community between believers, and the mission make for a powerful defense as they converge on the field of ministry.*

On the other hand, the flight attendant has been trained. The training required to work as a flight attendant involves learning the emergency procedures for each aircraft and practicing those procedures. Flight attendants go through weeks of preparation for emergency landings, medical emergencies in the air, and how to handle rowdy passengers. They have been trained with the knowledge of what might happen and how to handle it.

Too many churches rely on surface-level orientation. They operate as if a periodic explanation of what might happen is enough for the members to fulfill the mission of the church. Training that moves a church into transformational practices does much more. Training focuses on matters of the heart. Orientation is from experts and assumes everything about those being trained. Training is from people on a journey together. Orientation operates on an "inform and release" mentality that abandons people. Training focuses on real-time behavior, readying a person for likely circumstances, proper motives for action, and building proper expectations. Orientation is often done with a book and creates a modern Gnostic. Training is done life-on-life and produces a disciple preparing to disciple others.

Strong training in TCs includes stories from the field. People who are engaging the mission of God tell their experiences. Apprentice relationships are ideal for those learning how to engage other people in the mission of God. Above all an environment of training keeps the conversation about the mission going. TC believers are also made aware of resources that will help them in real time as they join God on mission. Telling the story of what is happening in the community and world creates an environment designed to guard people from being alone in following God's will. Training in TCs stresses the need to engage the mission as a community of believers rather than solo operators. Through effective training, it takes believers off the church campus and sends them together onto the mission field of the surrounding community together.

Better systems of training and deployment affect the bottom line measurements: lives transformed for Jesus Christ.

Training is varied. Transformational Churches prepare people to reach people for Christ in a wide variety of ways. Most of them create organic environments that include ongoing conversations. Conversations address subjects like who they are engaging and how they are engaging them. Pastor Jason Allison believes evangelism can be an awkward experience in the lives of Christians. He believes that inspiring and equipping people for evangelism are critical. He told about a particular Sunday service when he pulled up a stool and said, "All right, if you are going to learn how to share your faith, what do you need from me?" Pastor Allison said that he felt the congregation responded well and benefited by his open-ended approach.

Transformational leaders tell stories of their personal involvement and efforts to touch people far from God. Modeling how to engage people far from God in relationships is a key strategy. They understand that they had the same responsibility to engage people far from God as did the church members. When the people hear the stories of disciple making from the leaders, then they are more likely to engage in the work themselves.

Pastor Manuel Dorado has established a small-group outreach culture at Temple Rosade Sharon in Salinas, California. Small groups have social events that are designed for inviting new people. Their women's small groups will have a "makeover" night to provide a comfortable social environment to meet new people. Groups celebrate birthdays or have meals monthly for the purpose of inviting new people. Pastor Dorado said, "It's all relational and building relationships. We use the Luke 10 model: bless people in their homes, meet their felt needs, and when their hearts are ready and open, you give the full message of the gospel. Peers, coworkers, and family members begin to come in."

Other TCs are more intentional about the training and environments to reach people. Vaughn Forest Church in Montgomery, Alabama, has implemented an intentional process written by their pastor. Pastor Lawrence Phipps has been involved in just about every major evangelism training process over the years. He wanted to design something that would "disciple people to share their faith, connect those people to small groups, and provide ongoing one-on-one or one-on-two discipleship relationships." The process is called LIFE. Pastor Phipps wanted disciples to learn how to share faith as part of their lifestyle, not just through designated church visitation times.

Preparing believers to make disciples was an obvious priority for the TCs we discovered through our study. Though their methods varied, it serves as an invaluable tool for moving members from campus gatherings to mission in the community and world.

The third step to engaging in God's mission is providing personal leadership to believers. Most of us live in an ocean of digital information. But can individuals be equipped through e-mail, iPods, and Webinars alone? Is it possible for individual people on mission to find answers as problems and challenges arise? Perhaps, to some extent, the answer is yes. But raw data from impersonal mechanisms can only take you so far. This thinking applies to programs as well.

As much as systems and processes are critical to the mission of a local church, there can be a downside. Human beings need other human beings in order for true growth to occur. The most valuable resources for the missional journey are real-life examples and real-time conversations. Transformational Churches create mission-deployment environments populated with people for personal, informal conversations and relationships.

The apostle Paul had a credible missionary resume. He considered the gospel something that was given to him by God and that God trusted him to live out. Additionally, he understood the task of giving a personal example of it as well to the church. Paul's story was inspirational because his faith went beyond explaining religious words and ideas. People witnessed Paul in action as a model for the mission. He took God's confidence in him seriously. Paul instructed the Philippian Christians to "do what you have learned and received and heard and seen in me, and the God of peace will be with you" (Phil. 4:9). God has given us the responsibility to be a living example of Christ.

People on mission need godly examples to follow. Because our journey with Christ is constantly turning onto new paths, we cannot count on yesterday's growth to suffice for today. Sadly, many Christians live for years off of spiritual leftovers. One of the main culprits for living this way is the lack of solid examples in their lives. Without a teacher to guide them into the mission of God, believers miss the fresh lessons necessary to keep on being transformed by the power of Christ. People who are coming to Christ with no church background (which is more and more the case) need to witness real Christianity lived out.

Whatever term you like to use—teacher, mentor, coach—they are necessary to equip people to live on mission. In TCs, we found that the activity of community converged with the value of vibrant leadership to provide the necessary environment to help believers move out into the mission of the church. Having someone farther ahead on the journey keeps the less mature Christian from becoming stagnant.

> *The most valuable resource for the missional journey is real-life examples and real-time conversations.*

Paul and Timothy are examples of this relationship. "My true child in the faith" was how Paul addressed Timothy (1 Tim. 1:2). Paul gave plenty of encouragement and advice to the young pastor. Today you may find your need to be a "Paul" to a new Christian. Perhaps you are a "Timothy" who needs to seek out a more mature believer to guide you through the mission. No matter where you are in the mission, make sure you are participating in it within a community of faith that nurtures transformation. Mentoring serves to fulfill an important portion of the mission—making disciples. Mentoring is essential for encouraging people on mission with God.

The fourth step for engaging in God's mission is moving into the community. Often when doing consulting with a church, a touchy subject arises. It comes about because of a simple question: Do any of the people who live in the homes directly adjacent to the church property attend the church? More often than not, the answer is no. For one reason or another, the neighbors see the church as a nuisance, in the way, a source of noise, or lowering their property value. Whatever the reason, churches seem to struggle with building a good reputation in the community. TCs are just the opposite. Instead of waiting for the neighbors to come to them, they choose to go out and meet the neighbors.

TCs build a good reputation with the city. Their determination to work for the good of the community changes the perception of who they are. Covenant Fellowship launched in Willis, Texas, (fifty miles north of Houston) in 2000. The dream of brothers Sean and Heath Cook was to impact people with the message of God's love through a local church. The dream resulted in the establishment of a Transformational Church. On numerous occasions the fellowship has been recognized by the mayor and Willis City Council for their community involvement. Community projects have included:

> *Trash Off:* An annual event where everybody in the community can bring all their trash to roll away dumpsters as church volunteers help clean up the community.
>
> *Crawford's Corner Park Remodel:* Church volunteers built a gazebo, installed new equipment including a water fountain, and hosted a ribbon-cutting ceremony.
>
> *Willis City Entrance Upgrade:* Church volunteers installed and landscaped a fifty-foot flagpole and "welcome to Willis" sign.
>
> *Tender Loving Care Food Pantry:* Covenant Fellowship organized a collaborative effort to minister to the needy in an area with thirty thousand residents. Thirteen other churches are

involved. Other community partners include the Salvation Army, local news stations, grocery stores, and schools.

Covenant Fellowship practices "Equipping Communities" as part of their purpose. They believe, "Responsible leaders, who embrace the courage and resolve to make a difference, will become the heartbeat and passion of our communities."

Look at this following statement from our survey of TCs:

- "Our church has earned a good reputation among city leaders by meeting needs." (64 percent strongly or moderately agree)

What accounts for this response? Transformational Churches engage the community with great passion and with a vision to change the fabric of their community. Rather than holding out the old "come and gather" mentality, they have embraced the "go and tell" commands of Jesus. The churches choosing transformation as their goal know that it cannot be done "in house." We noticed that in TCs, the church celebrated mission endeavors that blessed and transformed the community as well as celebrating ministry that built up the local church. However, in the comparison churches the vast majority of celebration was focused on internal ministry engagement. The TCs felt like a movement into the city while the comparison churches felt like an institution seeking self-preservation.

Consider these two scenarios:

Cornerstone Church has a full calendar of activities for their members and the campus to go along with it. They report a growing number in attendance from year to year. For decades they have invested resources into an attractive sanctuary, effective signage, strong children's ministries, building a recreation center, and sending people on short-term mission trips to far-flung places around the globe. With regularity they hold evangelism training courses on Monday nights to educate believers in presenting the gospel and send them out for visitation to prospects. The church regularly sees visitors but seems to retain few of them. The church is puzzled as to why their attendance seems to increase marginally from year to year but the number of baptisms flatlined many years ago.

Ten miles away is Riverview Church. Riverview is not completely unlike Cornerstone in size and rate of attendance growth. They hold worship services each Sunday morning, and much of the church is engaged in Bible studies. The building is not as fancy, more utilitarian looking from the street. The activities of the church as listed in the church calendar seem less than one would expect from a growing church. Formal evangelism training is rarely offered, but the leaders of the church speak about and model sharing their faith often. Sharing Christ is a central value. The emphasis placed on ministry with Riverview is not based on the location of the church campus but the location of the church members. The push to get people serving is not always in the church programs but oftentimes with the church in the community. The church is consistent to report the number in attendance at worship and Bible study, but the people love to hear stories of lives changed through simple acts of service and witnessing. Annually, the church sees growth in the number of new believers at the church and feels an excitement about the future. The leaders of the church know the leaders of the city and have forged solid friendships through which they personally share their faith.

These two fictional churches are composite stories of the churches we surveyed in the Transformational Church study. Maybe you feel like your church was being described as one or the other. But what was the difference we found between the two congregations? The difference is the "where" of mission. Too many churches limit their ministry to the acreage upon which their building rests. To be transformational, a church must constantly commission their people into service for the city to display and tell the gospel.

- "When our church serves in the local city or community, we look for opportunities to share the message of Christ." (75 percent strongly or moderately agree)

TCs are intentionally looking for ways to engage with the community at large. Believers understand that the mission is "out there" and not "in here." Leaders must decide to train believers not just in an evangelistic presentation but in a missional lifestyle. Evangelism training is part of preparing for God's mission but not living it. Service is a portion of God's mission but not all of it. God's mission must be lived out each day as believers live out their daily routines. In TCs the mission of God is so apparently active among the people of the church that the city misses them when they are not around.

TC members are comfortable sharing their faith. The mission of God does not progress unless people are talking about God's mission to save. The talk goes deeper than the theology of mission or the way things ought to be. We need to talk about the subject of God's mission. Paul said in 2 Corinthians 5:20, "Therefore, we are ambassadors for Christ; certain that God is appealing through us, we plead on Christ's behalf, 'Be reconciled to God.'" The work of the Christian is to talk about what is on God's heart, namely the redemption of man.

> *Leaders must decide to train believers not just in an evangelistic presentation but in a missional lifestyle.*

- "Our church's members understand the importance of sharing their faith story with friends." (77 percent strongly or moderately agree)

The churches that showed a transformational practice in the area of mission were filled with believers who shared their faith naturally. As you can see from the statistics above, 77 percent of the members in these churches understood the importance of sharing their faith story. The overwhelming response came when dealing with their personal story of faith and not an evangelistic outline previously memorized. Now we can make an educated assumption that many believers in these churches have learned different gospel presentations which they employ at different levels of their disciple-making efforts. But the emphasis we find is that members in TCs find it to be natural to share the gospel in a personal way in the context of relationships.

Jason Allison is founding pastor of Tera Nova Community Church in Delaware, Ohio. Jason lives like a missionary. Telling stories to people already in his church is an important way to equip them for evangelism according to Pastor Allison. "I tell story after story of me hanging out with unchurched people in Delaware. The guy who cuts my hair, his wife is an atheist and they came to church two weeks ago. . . . In the process of my teaching, I will say, 'Oh, by the way, I just shared the gospel.'"

The lesson to be learned here is obvious: transformation of individuals and communities happens at the same pace as the gospel is proclaimed. Our churches need once again to be populated with people who enjoy sharing the good news of Christ. If you find your church filled with cowardly Christians or apathetic ambassadors, the elements of vibrant leadership and prayerful dependence need to kick into gear. The transformation of lives from lost to found is waiting on us.

> *TCs have moved their membership from the "pay, pray, and get out of the way" mentality to a "go, tell, and show" obsession.*

TCs have broken the missionary/professional clergy caste-sytem and placed the mission into the hands of all believers. And it should not surprise the church today—though it does—when believers respond to the task of being on mission. Why? Because God has made us to be on mission. The new life imparted to us is one that begs to be shared. TCs have moved their membership from the "pay, pray, and get out of the way" mentality to a "go, tell, and show" obsession. When we do for people what God has called them to do, everyone gets hurt and the mission is hindered. The Transformational Church is one that sets its people loose on mission because the people want to be out there.

Conclusion

Transformational Churches multiply vibrant missionaries for the harvest. Missionaries understand who they are and why they do what they do. TCs establish motivation and training to aid their missionary members.

What kind of environment helps cultivate vibrant missionaries? Paul compares his care for the Thessalonians as a mother taking care of children. The caring environment experienced by children should be illustrative of how we lead and aid one another in our churches.

Right now your church may feel like the nursery—lots of needy believers centered on their own needs. Or perhaps it looks more like a high school with people all trying to discover themselves, test the boundaries of freedom, and set a course for life. TCs have created a setting where the mature are encouraged to lead the immature. They help the immature to see where they are missing the mission. Leadership is established along the lines of helping people see and participate in the mission rather than stagnate at one phase of development.

Rick Carlson, pastor of River of Life Fellowship, Wellington, Colorado, found an incredible mission opportunity by becoming a volunteer high school girls basketball coach in his community. Although his team won only three games, the example and payoff for the gospel was great. Almost every one of the girls is now a part of the church youth group. The girls in his church do not know whether to call him coach or pastor. Most of them call him coach. Their parents do not attend, but these formerly unchurched high school girls met a believer who entered their world instead of expecting them to come to his first.

People come into the body of Christ constantly. But in a TC the influence is on moving people from *new to the mission* to *active on mission* to *leader in the mission.* Churches that simply chase the next big thing will create confused children in the family. Close relationships and clear vision help produce missionary members who actively share good news through word and deed.

But a certain struggle remains—that the heart is an idol factory. Many pastors and church leaders fall prey to their own whims. Becoming frustrated with a lack of commitment by the people

> *Pastors too often consider themselves as "religious professionals who can put on a show" rather than people transformed and sent on mission.*

in the church, they begin looking for secondary and tertiary measurements to justify their own work. Ultimately they begin worshipping their own work. Pastors too often consider themselves as "religious professionals who can put on a show" rather than people transformed and sent on mission.

> *Transformational Churches multiply vibrant missionaries for the harvest.*

Our nature will get us in deep trouble with God and our ministries if left unchecked.

The people in our churches may not be living out a missionary lifestyle because they have yet to see anyone live that way. Leaders should not get angry but get right with the Lord and become a missionary example to the people. In his letters Paul continued to point to his example lived out among the people. He was not angry because of their lack of responsiveness. He continued like a good lawyer to point to the evidence. The evidence was his modeling of the Christian life.

We must resist the pull of idols (success and recognition) and live the mission to make reality everything about His will for the world. Knowing what we ought to do and be for Jesus Christ is not enough. Paul confessed that what he knew in his head and heart often did not produce the desired results, "For I know that nothing good lives in me, that is, in my flesh. For the desire to do what is good is with me, but there is no ability to do it" (Rom. 7:18). God must work deeper in us to help us become what He wants. Being a disciple maker is often confused with a task versus a person. We often focus on the work. A missional lifestyle that bears transformation at the greatest level of influence is not *do* but *be*. Girls basketball coach-pastor Rick Carlson is an example of being a missionary concerned with transformation. Transformational Christians are filled with believers whose lives are marked by serving and sharing. End of discussion.

Mission is the opposite of self. We have to remember to make it about God and not about us. So, what is the foundation of this deeper transformational life when someone is not *doing* the missionary lifestyle but *being* missionary? Jesus explained: "In the same way, let your light shine before men, so that they may see your good works and give glory to your Father in heaven" (Matt. 5:16). We let our lights shine for a purpose greater than high attendance at Sunday School or maximum participation in the church cleanup day. Those are by-products. Loving people unconditionally and serving them like Jesus will cause them to look to the Father. Then, transformation can occur in their lives.

Mission is the opposite of self.

Our transformational lifestyle must be compelled by love. "For Christ's love compels us, since we have reached this conclusion: if One died for all, then all died. And He died for all so that those who live should no longer live for themselves, but for the One who died for them and was raised" (2 Cor. 5:14–15). To *compel* is to be "under the influence." Being influenced by the character and nature of God will lead us to join His mission of transforming people to be like Christ, congregations to act like the body of Christ, and communities to mirror the kingdom of God.

10
Not the Final Word

And Jesus responded, "Simon son of Jonah, you are blessed because flesh and blood did not reveal this to you, but My Father in heaven. And I also say to you that you are Peter, and on this rock I will build My church, and the forces of Hades will not overpower it."

(Matthew 16:17–18)

The Best Endings

Sometimes the best part of a story is the end, especially when you are telling the story to a child. Once the hero has arrived, the enemy defeated, and all is made right, then comes the ending. One of the things we've found as dads is that the best endings are not endings at all. The best endings are the "they lived happily ever after" ones. It gives the sense that the book is done but the story is not.

We hope to leave you with a sense that even though the book is ending, the story is continuing with Transformational Churches. After more than a year of survey work, months of interpreting data, and the journey of writing this book—we just don't believe the story is over. In fact, from the wonderful churches we met along the way, we are sure it is not.

Where We Started

We have written a lot about the church. We have taught even more classes and conferences. And the sermons—we lost count many years ago. But we do it because we love the church.

The last few years have tested our hope for the church. As we have worked so closely to the statistics, certain days were filled with more statistical despair than either of us cared for. But through it all, we know that the truth about the church is greater than what we can see in the church right now. At least in most of the North American church.

Perhaps that is why we are now once again energized about the church. Though we have seen and reported our share of the difficulties, a new story is ready to be told. It is the story of hope that has been shown in the pages you have read. It is the hope that more and more churches are committing themselves to live out a transformational ministry.

As we entered into the Transformational Church study, we wondered what new discoveries would be made. Ultimately, the best discovery made has been the churches where lives are changed with regularity. We came face-to-face with pastors and members who care more for the kingdom's mission than their own personal needs. With joy we saw churches transforming entire communities with the gospel.

What Jesus Thinks of the Church

Jesus told us what He thought of the church.

"But you," He asked them, "who do you say that I am?" Simon Peter answered, "You are the Messiah, the Son of the living God!" And Jesus responded, "Simon son of Jonah, you are blessed because flesh and blood did not reveal this to you, but My Father in heaven. And I also say to you that you are Peter, and on this rock I will build My church, and the forces of Hades will not overpower it." (Matt. 16:15–18)

The church is built upon a different foundation than we often see in the modern church. Sure, everyone has the best of intentions, but we often fall short. Jesus clearly taught that the church would be built on the "rock" of Peter's confession. Better yet, it is built upon God's revelation that led to Peter's confession.

We both advocate that churches minister in a culturally comprehensible manner. But before we think about the culture, we must first be biblically grounded. And being biblically grounded means that the church is centered on God's revelation of Jesus as the Messiah.

> *It is the hope that more and more churches are committing themselves to live out a transformational ministry.*

Transformational Churches know the Source of transformation. They do not fall into the trap of believing in personal innovation or corporate vision as the source of changed lives. Focusing on Christ, they show and share the gospel. Focusing on Christ, believers confidently live knowing that many more lives will be transformed.

So much today seems to shroud the work of the church. Distracted by pedestrian logistics, some churches become mired in minutiae. Falling into sin, others disqualify themselves from authentic ministry. Transformational Churches on the other hand remain clearly focused on the Messiah who founded and loves the church.

Jesus states that He will build His church. As much as we want to help, He simply doesn't need it. But He still invites us into the task with Him.

In 1 Corinthians 12:18, Paul taught that the Spirit places the church together as He wills. The churches we discovered who are making a transformational impact in their communities are convinced of this scriptural principle. Carrying a belief that you belong there (wherever *there* is for you) is critical to engaging in God's mission. Members and leaders of TCs live convinced that God has put them together for this mission.

They believe that Christ is busy in their midst, building a church for His glory, the good of the city, for calling the lost to salvation and the believer to a thriving relationship with the King.

Unafraid and Unashamed

When Jesus spoke to Peter, He promised that the forces of Hades could not prevail against the church. We wonder how many churches really believe that statement. Most churches agree with it theologically but not practically. The churches we saw transforming their communities don't just believe it. They live in the midst of the words of Jesus.

The discovery of these everyday churches transforming lives gives us hope because they are on the mission we can all join. The churches that act more like an evangelical version of the Amish community obviously do not believe in the prevailing power of the church. Their fortress mentality betrays a fear of the community and what the mission might bring to their door.

Focusing on Christ, they show and share the gospel.

Churches delivering transformation embrace the prevailing power of Jesus. They engage the mission of God unafraid and unashamed. We believe the Transformational Church has the ability from Christ to serve locally, plant nationally, and reach unreached people groups globally. They step out ready for the next part of the story, knowing that adventure awaits.

The Differentiating Factor

Throughout the study and consequently in this book, we saw the three framework principles differentiating most churches from those in the TC category. Remember from the discussion of the Transformational Loop in chapter 2 that the three framework principles are Connection, Catharsis, and Convergence.

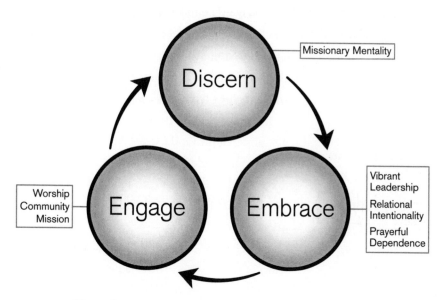

Transformational Loop: The New Scorecard

We invite you to jump into the loop. First, find your connection point. It is not just one thing. There is no mandate for you to start at prayer or leadership or any other particular element of the Loop. Rather, carefully assess the church and find the place where you can most easily get involved in God's mission. It could come through highlighting a ministerial strength in the church or repenting of a sinful practice. If you are a leader, pick an element where God is working and jump in without fear.

Second, prepare for a cathartic experience. In fact, work for it. The experience does not have to be overly dramatic. It could simply be the decision that you are tired of decline and a lack of impact on people's lives. Too many churches look around and know they should change but never have the will to do so. Don't wait until a dramatic event is necessary to move the church into action. Decide that now is the time. This is the moment when transformation takes hold of the church afresh.

> *Churches engage the mission of God unafraid and unashamed.*

Third, remember that the elements taught in this book are not distinct principles from one another. The Christian life is one of constant interplay. Believers are interdependent on one another. When the Spirit is active in one part of the body, He is active in all of the body. If leadership becomes vibrant, it will be because of prayerful dependence. If the church is prayerful, we will better understand God's heart for humankind and develop a sharper missionary mentality. Though we should endeavor to understand every aspect of the Christian life, we must not isolate their practice and effect.

> *Regrettably, it has become acceptable to sit in church week after week and do nothing but call yourself a follower of Christ.*

Stretching out before you is hope because God is not finished with you or the church you serve. He passionately longs to guide your church from its places of struggle to the sure footing found in Christ. God knows the hope that awaits the leader and member that trusts His Son to overpower the forces of death, hell, and the grave.

The Living Goal

We love the church. Our focus and ministry is now to do research and provide resources for local churches. We have learned that resources and research are tools, not the goal. Transformed people changing the world for Jesus' kingdom is the goal! That's why we minister in and through local churches.

Regrettably, it has become acceptable to sit in church week after week and do nothing but call yourself a follower of Christ. It is time to put this Laodicean notion to bed forever in the Western church. We must work for nothing less than the church's mission to see people transformed to look like Christ, churches to act like the body of Christ, and communities changed to reflect the kingdom of God. The living goal of the church must be the living Christ alive in others.

It can and will happen when we take the gospel seriously for the transformational power it has. Our churches should never preach any message that would not be true if Jesus had not died on the cross. It is great to be practical in what we teach, but if we hesitate to share about the work of Christ, what good is it? Using practical messages can help us share biblical truth, but ultimately our goal is that people leave with the truth, not just true stuff. The truth is the person of Jesus.

The Story Continues

In concluding The Chronicles of Narnia with the book *The Last Battle*, C. S. Lewis ends the story this way:

> And as He [Aslan] spoke, He no longer looked to them like a lion; but the things that began to happen after that were so great and beautiful that I cannot write them. And for us this is the end of all the stories, and we can most truly say that they all live happily ever after. But for them it was only the beginning of the real story. All their life in this world and all their adventures in Narnia had only been the cover and the title page: now at last they were beginning Chapter One of the Great Story which no one on earth has read: which goes on for ever: in which every chapter is better than the one before.[1]

We hope that you have just read the cover and title page for a new journey of transformation. The book you are about to complete is merely moving you into "Chapter One of the Great Story which no one on earth has read" of what the Christ is about to do in your church. The God who fashioned the universe and formed the church is ready to deliver hope to you again. He is refining the way we view church and the transformation that comes from gospel-centered, repentance-filled lives.

> *Stretching out before you is hope because God is not finished with you or the church you serve.*

More and more we are convinced that God is preparing to do a new and reviving work in the Western church. Our prayer is that of Paul's for the Ephesians.

> Now to Him who is able to do above and beyond all that we ask or think—according to the power that works in you—to Him be glory in the church and in Christ Jesus to all generations, forever and ever. Amen. (Eph. 3:20–21)

We hope that you find yourself in the midst of God's Transformational Church that is beyond all that you can ask or imagine.

APPENDIX

TRANSFORMATIONAL CHURCH
RESEARCH METHODOLOGY

ONE OF THE MOST important tests of the value of a survey is the "sniff test." We all learned this test from our mothers. Mothers have a highly developed sense of smell and could tell with one whiff when we hadn't taken a bath, been around someone who had been smoking, and even know what we had been eating.

In the same way research must pass the sniff test. Both the results and how the research was conducted need to make sense and not hint at any bias when the reader gets a whiff.

From the beginning we decided to be transparent about this study's methodology. So at several stages along the way, we sought out expert advice to test our process. Providing an open process not only made for a better study; it also should allow participants and you the reader to have confidence in the work throughout every phase. Keep in mind—if someone won't tell you how they know, you might wonder if they really do know.

Here is the process we used to develop and test the Transformational Church research and assessment tool.

Phase 1: Identify Churches for Deeper Learning

The first step of the research was a quantitative research study of Protestant churches. Among the first seven thousand pastors who completed the quantitative survey, their churches were from 123 different denominations as indicated from our sample. Within the survey we had a shorter list to choose from which showed that 6 percent of participants were non-denominational (or had no connection with a denomination-like affinity group, such as Independent Fundamentalist networks). The goal was to establish benchmarks of key metrics but more importantly to identify the best churches. These churches would be the source of additional insights in Phase 2.

> *Both the results and how the research was conducted need to make sense and not hint at any bias when the reader gets a whiff.*

A calling list was randomly drawn from a list of all Protestant churches in the United States of America. Up to six calls were made to reach a sampled phone number. Each interview was conducted with the senior pastor, minister, or priest of the church called. The calling was done in waves of one thousand completed interviews working through a portion of the sample in each wave systematically with quotas for church size (sizes of the churches were proportional to the normal size of U.S. churches). The calling was done by a professional call center with experienced supervision.

After analyzing survey responses, we used the following criteria to determine the most effective churches among the 4,006 churches that were interviewed in the first four waves of Phase 1. To aid in recruiting churches for Phase 3, a total of seven thousand pastors ultimately completed Phase 1 questions.

- The pastor must strongly agree that "our church considers Scripture to be the authority for our church and our lives."
- The church must have grown at least 10 percent comparing the churches current worship attendance to five years prior.

- Because of the volatility in church growth numbers among small churches (e.g., one family coming or going has a large impact on percentage growth), the church must have a minimum of fifty in current worship attendance.
- The church could not have more than one missing response among the ten questions in the survey.
- The church gave us permission to contact them for further research on church health.
- The remaining criterion was a score based on rankings on each of the following seven areas:

1. Percent growth in worship attendance (current vs. five years prior).
2. Percent of worship attendance involved in some small group, Sunday School class, or similar group.
3. New commitments per attendee (new commitments to Jesus Christ as Savior through your church in the past twelve months divided by current average worship attendance).
4. Percent of new commitments to Jesus Christ who have also become active in the life of your church (last twelve months).
5. Percent of adults who attend your church at least once a month who have regular responsibilities at your church.
6. Percent of adults who attend your church at least once a month who are involved in ministries or projects that serve people in your community not affiliated with your church.
7. Level of agreement with the statement, "We are consistently hearing reports of changed lives at our church."

As you can tell, we were looking to change the scorecard. We were not saying that things like attendance and conversations don't matter—they do! But they are not the only things that matter. For too long we have focused only on nickels, noses, and numbers. We wanted to look at lives changed, churches growing, and communities being changed and served. Hence, we started with a new scorecard and some expanded metrics.

Phase 2: Qualitative Research
to Obtain In-depth Insights

We then contacted the 298 churches with the best responses based on the Phase 1 criteria and requested to interview the senior pastor, in person if at all possible. With much persistence by LifeWay church consultants, more than 250 interviews were completed, as they traveled to meet pastors and church leaders from Maine to California, from Washington to Florida.

The basis of the interview was a pair of topic guides that the interviewer used to encourage each pastor to describe the activities of the church, why it is working, and how they know it is effective. Because of the depth required in the interviews, the nine general subject areas were split between the two topic guides. Most interviews used only one, but a few generous pastors were interviewed using both.

Each pastor was given the opportunity to provide additional facets of ministry they considered vital to an effective ministry. The additional information provided learning beyond the general areas of inquiry that included worship, evangelism, discipleship, small groups, prayer, leadership, how new people are connected, the quality of life within a congregation, and level of engaging a lost and hurting world.

The interviewers employed by LifeWay in the process were church consultants that had extensive ministry experience. To prepare each consultant and to ensure that each interview was carried out in a consistent manner, two training sessions were provided for conducting interviews.

Each interview was recorded and transcribed. Each church consultant completed a summary immediately following the interview highlighting the most important things they heard. We were able to enhance the interview quality by sharing the early transcripts among church consultants for them to hear other interviewers and observe when useful information was obtained and when it was missed.

Interviewer observations and analysis of the transcripts yielded principles that have shaped this book and provided many practical examples.

Phase 3: Church Assessment

Principles that were common among the top 10 percent churches were used to develop questions for the church assessment tool. We (Thom and Ed) and our LifeWay Research Team (particularly Scott McConnell and Lizette Beard) looked at them extensively.

The questions were reviewed by a panel of experts that included:

- Alan Hirsch, founding director of Forge Mission Training Network and author of *The Forgotten Ways* and coauthor of *Untamed* with his wife Debra
- Chuck Lawless, dean of the Billy Graham School of Missions and Evangelism at the Southern Baptist Theological Seminary, author of *Discipled Warriors*
- Elmer Towns, cofounder of Liberty University, author of more than one hundred titles listed in the Library of Congress including *The Names of the Holy Spirit* and *11 Innovations in the Local Church*
- Bob Whitesel, professor at Indiana Wesleyan University, consultant with Creative Church Consulting International and author of *Spiritual Waypoints* and *Inside the Organic Church*
- Bill Easum, senior consultant of 21st Century Strategies and author of *A Second Resurrection* and *Go Big with Small Groups* among many other books
- Gary McIntosh, professor of Christian Ministry and Leadership at Talbot School of Theology and author of thirteen books including *Here Today, There Tomorrow: Unleashing Your Church's Potential* and *Beyond the First Visit: The Complete Guide to Connecting Guests to Your Church*
- Eric Geiger, executive pastor of Christ Fellowship (Miami, Florida) and author of *Identity* and coauthor *of Simple Church*
- Dallas Anderson, national facilitator of evangelism for the Mission America Coalition and director of proclamation ministries for the Billy Graham Center

An extensive list of questions was chosen initially—twenty questions each for the seven elements of the Transformational Loop—140 questions in all. The lengthy survey was used so that the paring down of the survey would be based on objective criteria rather than the opinions of a few.

A random set of Protestant churches was then invited to have their pastor and adult members use the Transformational Church assessment tool.

Analysis was done on 4,077 members who completed the initial version of the survey. Subsequent analysis was done on another 11,000 completed member surveys on the same and/or modified versions throughout the research process. The analysis validated the scales. In each element outliers constituted 1 percent or less of the values.

Factor analysis was run on each element of the survey. Cronbach's Alpha for each factor proved very reliable with the lowest being .826. This internal consistency establishes the reliability of the questions in the assessment tool. Individual questions that did not have at least 10 percent of values on each half of the Likert scale were eliminated, as were questions that did not load with a factor in their section. The final set of eighty-two questions comprised the assessment tool.

As of the print date of this manuscript, 280 randomly selected Protestant churches were recruited to test the validity of the final assessment tool including completed surveys from more than twenty thousand individual church members.

Conclusion

In the end we are confident that the principles discovered among effective churches were assembled in a reliable survey. The principles included in Transformational Church have been and continue to be rigorously tested. Additionally, the assessment tool produced by the study is both internally and externally valid.

As we conclude the writing of this book, the Transformational Church study is ongoing. In fact, we expect it will continue for the next few years.

Every time a church participates in the assessment tool, we hope to learn a little bit more about how a church can be an instrument of transformation in the community.

(The numbers are accurate as of March 29, 2010.)

NOTES

Chapter 1

1. Jim Herrington, *Transformation: The Bottom Line from City Reaching: On the Road to Community Transformation* (Pasadena, CA: William Carey Publishers, 1999), 106.
2. Malcolm McDow and Alvin Reid, *Firefall: How God Has Shaped History Through Revivals* (Nashville, TN: B&H Publishing Group, 1997), 278.
3. Francis Chan, *Crazy Love: Overwhelmed by a Relentless God* (Colorado Springs, CO: David C. Cook, 2008), 180.

Chapter 2

1. Reggie McNeal, *Missional Renaissance* (San Francisco, CA: Jossey-Bass, 2009), 16.
2. Ibid.
3. Ibid., 42.
4. Ibid., 68.

Chapter 3

1. Alan Hirsch, *Forgotten Ways: Reactivating the Missional Church* (Grand Rapids, MI: Brazos Press, 2006), 129.
2. Stephen Neill, *Creative Tension* (London: Edinburgh House Press, 1959), 81.
3. Leonard Sweet, *SoulTsunami: Sink or Swim in New Millennium Culture* (Grand Rapids, MI: Zondervan Publishing House, 1999), 50.

Chapter 4

1. See http://www.charismachurch.com/charismax/welcome (accessed 3-29-2010).
2. Tri Robinson, *Revolutionary Leadership: Building Momentum in Your Church through the Synergy Cycle* (Norcross, GA: Ampelon Publishing, 2005), 30.

   3. See http://www.msnbc.msn.com/id/10154383 (accessed 1-22-2010).
   4. Albert L. Winseman, Donald O. Clifton, and Curt Liesveld, *Living your Strengths: Discover your God-given Talents and Inspire Your Community* (New York, NY: Gallup Press 2004), ix.
   5. Jay McSwain, e-mail correspondence, 11-9-2009.

Chapter 5

   1. Tony Stoltzfus, *Leadership Coaching: The Discipline, Skills, and Heart of a Christian Church* (BookSurge Publishing, 2005).
   2. Bob Logan and Tara Miller, *From Followers to Leaders* (St. Charles, IL: ChurchSmart Resources, 2007), 20.
   3. Neal McGlohon, Personal Interview, 11/19/2009.
   4. Tim Keller, *The Prodigal God: Recovering the Heart of the Christian Faith* (New York, NY: Penguin Group, 2008), 124–25.

Chapter 6

   1. Jim Cymbala, *Fresh Wind, Fresh FireWhat Happens When God's Spirit Invades The Hearts of His People* (Grand Rapids, MI: Zondervan Publishing House, 1997), 19.
   2. Iain Murray, *Revival and Revivalism: The Making and Marring of American Evangelicalism, 1750–1858* (Edinburg: Banner of Truth Trust, 1995), 17.
   3. Wayne Cordeiro, *The Divine Mentor: Growing Your Faith as You Sit at the Feet of the Savior* (Bloomington, MN: Bethany House Publishers, 2007), 62.
   4. Jim Cymbala, *Fresh Wind, Fresh Fire: What Happens When God's Spirit Invades The Hearts of His People* (Grand Rapids, MI: Zondervan Publishing House, 1997), 50.
   5. David Garrison, *Church Planting Movements: How God Is Redeeming A Lost World* (Midlothian, VA: WIGtake Resources, 2004), 176–77.
   6. Leonard Ravenhill, *Why Revival Tarries* (Mineapolis, MN: Bethany House Publishers, 1988), 23.

Chapter 7

   1. Henry Blackaby, *Created to be God's Friend: How God Shapes Those He Loves* (Nashville, TN: Thomas Nelson, 2005), 83.
   2. David T. Olson, *The American Church in Crisis* (Grand Rapids, MI: Zondervan, 2008), 180.
   3. George Barna, *Revolution* (Carol Stream, IL: Tyndale House Publishers, 2006), 49.

4. Matt Redman compiler, *The Heart of Worship Files* (Ventura, CA: Regal Books, 2003), 31.
5. J. Oswald Sanders, "Intimacy is Nourished by Worship," *Knowing and Doing*, Winter 2006, C. S. Lewis Institute, 1.
6. See http://www.redeemer.com/sundays/worship_and_music (accessed 10/12/2009).

Chapter 8

1. Bob Logan and Tara Miller, *From Followers to Leaders* (Churchsmart Resources, 2008), 205.
2. Although churches and homes remain the most popular venues for small group meetings, these communities can thrive in other venues as well. *Simple Church* coauthor Eric Geiger and LifeWay's David Francis conducted an analysis of the four hundred "vibrant" churches identified in *Simple Church* and discovered that 87.5 percent offered Sunday School—or its functional on-campus equivalent by another name—as the primary small-group strategy, with most of the remainder operating home-based small groups.
3. E-mail correspondence 1-27-2010.
4. For a comprehensive treatment of *communitas*, see *The Forgotten Ways: Reactivating the Missional Church* by Alan Hisch (Grand Rapids, MI: Brazoa Press, 2006), 217–41).
5. See http://www.g12media.tv (accessed 3-29-2010).

Chapter 9

1. Rick Rusaw and Eric Swanson, *The Externally Focused Church* (Loveland, CO: Group Publishing, 2004).
2. See http://www.americanreligionsurvey-aris.org (accessed 1-27-2010).

Chapter 10

1. This is the final paragraph of the book *The Last Battle* by C. S. Lewis (New York, NY: HarperCollins, 2000).

Transform this book into action.

After reading this book, you might be asking *now what?* Here are a few common questions church leaders ask about implementing Transformational Church principles into their church. You can also check www.lifeway.com/tc for more detailed information, including updates, prices, and event and training dates.

How do I get my team up to speed on this quickly?

Convey the concepts in this book to your church leaders quickly, easily, and affordably using the *Transformational Church DVD Discussion Guide*. The kit includes a DVD and CD-ROM (with a listening guide) that leads your team through six sessions. Video from Thom Rainer, Ed Stetzer, Bruce Raley, and Philip Nation is featured in each session.

Is there a way to rally my team around the ideas of Transformational Church?

Treat your staff to a Transformational Church Pastor/Staff Retreat. Get everyone away from the distractions of daily church life. Use this dedicated time to grow and strengthen your team and to cast a shared vision for your church's future. The package includes content for discussion; sessions with speakers from the DVD videos; affinity groups with your peers; and time for your staff to meet and discuss the Transformational Church model and to plan its implementation for the unique environment of your church. And all of this is provided at a very affordable price. (Some details may change. Visit us online for the latest information.)

How do I assess where we are as a church and get our congregation thinking "Transformational"?

Before you can get where you want to go, you have to know where you are. The *Transformational Church Assessment Tool* (TCAT) can help. This online assessment uses a graded scale to gauge the perceptions of your church members concerning each of the seven Transformational Church elements. It can help you quickly assess where your church is strong now and areas that need development. Reports are updated in real time and are available throughout the survey process for your designated leaders to review at any time.

What if I'd like additional perspective on our church's assessment?

Many churches who go through the church assessment find it valuable to have a set of "outside eyes and ears" to guide them through the process. We have trained certified Transformational Church consultants specifically for this reason. They will visit your church personally, walk you through the assessment process, and propose the next steps to take based on your assessment results.

Can I help other churches become transformational?

We continue to train and certify Transformational Church Consultants to help church leaders take the assessment, analyze the results, and plan future actions to move toward transformation. If you're interested in serving as a consultant, visit www.lifeway.com/tc

www.lifeway.com/tc

LifeWay | Leadership